100
20TH -
CENTURY
SHOPS

100 20TH - CENTURY SHOPS

Edited by
Susannah Charlton
and Elain Harwood

BATSFORD

In memory of Elain Harwood
1958–2023

First published in the United Kingdom in 2023 by B.T. Batsford
43 Great Ormond Street
London WC1N 3HZ

An imprint of B.T. Batsford Holdings Limited

ISBN: 9781849947701

A CIP catalogue record for this book is available from the British Library.

10 9 8 7 6 5 4 3 2 1

Reproduction by Rival Colour Ltd, UK
Printed and bound by Toppan Leefung Ltd, China

This book can be ordered direct from the publisher at
www.batsfordbooks.com, or try your local bookshop.

MIX
Paper | Supporting
responsible forestry
FSC® C104723
FSC
www.fsc.org

CONTENTS

INTRODUCTION

What will be the future of shopping? Have we passed peak in-real-life shopping? Or will retailers and developers do ever more to lure us out to buy in person. What more can they dream up as a way to convince us that shopping is beyond a necessity but rather 'an experience', and an enjoyable social activity we can't do without? In 2022 I was a judge for the World Architecture Festival's Shopping award, and our winner was an enormous new complex just completed in Chengdu, China, which wraps shopping units around a completely fabricated 'ecological park featuring mountain and river scenery'. Other large-scale entries featured an Olympic-standard skateboard park, a rooftop Ferris wheel and a massive yellow Pikachu Pokémon figure. But alongside these was a suburban development in Melbourne, Australia, inspired by Queensgate Market, Huddersfield (1968–70 by the J. Seymour Harris Partnership) and an exquisitely detailed Japanese pavilion, which fused a spectacle shop with a bakery and a play area. Globally shopping seems to be alive and well, but perhaps significantly, there were no UK entries shortlisted.

The double impact of easy internet ordering, and the Covid pandemic, seems to have sucked some of the vitality out of the UK high street. The options offered by online browsing make even the most comprehensive department store look parochial. The knowing exclusivity of the 'curated' collections of exclusive boutiques have been at least partially supplanted by the social media posts of online influencers. Repeated doom-mongering, mass sell-offs (including that of the Debenhams chain) and bankruptcies, prompted the Twentieth Century Society both to launch our department stores campaign and to compile this book. We wanted to celebrate a world that seemed uniquely threatened, and to explore ways in which these buildings could be imaginatively repurposed. Before we go to press, the austerity crisis makes the future of many of these amazing buildings seem bleaker yet. But our belief that shops are important, not just for their architectural quality, but for the social histories they embody, has been strengthened by the enthusiasm of our members and supporters for the topic, and the extent of media interest.

Department stores in particular have been studied for their role in the emancipation of women, offering both an alternative employment to 'service', and a public venue in which women could be respectably visible and meet away from the scrutiny of home. But many of us also relate to our local department store extremely personally: it is the place we remember going to be fitted for our first shoes or bras, where we compiled wedding lists and purchased school uniforms, tried out double beds and then pushchairs, all of which speak to events that act as markers of major life milestones, both joyous and possibly traumatic. One of my earliest memories is of being lost among the rails in

RIGHT Marks & Spencer, Oxford Street, London by Trehearne and Norman with W.A. Lewis, 1929–30

Bentalls in Kingston. The planning inquiry into the future of the Marks & Spencer flagship building on Oxford Street captured the public imagination and put the environmental arguments in favour of adapting and reusing shopping buildings centre stage, albeit with an assumption that their higher floors might well be reasonably and more profitably switched to alternative uses, such as office or residential conversion. Here was a 'national treasure', a company with a much-voiced commitment to sustainability, set on sending a solid and reusable building to oblivion. It seemed to be an act that combined both a hypocritical disregard of those environmental credentials, and a deliberate lack of regard for its own popular heritage.

I don't really mourn the loss of shopping as a fun leisure activity. Maybe I was too scarred by the excruciating, sweaty embarrassment of Saturday afternoons wriggling on the floor of Top Shop and Miss Selfridge's claustrophobic communal changing rooms, trying to squeeze into skin-tight jeans in the pre-Lyra early 1980s. But I do remember the excitement of Eva Jiřičná's shops for Joseph, of their high-tech steel and glass, which felt unbelievably glamorous, and it was at the Katharine Hamnett Knightsbridge store, with its catwalk entrance way, that I first remember being aware of the work of Norman Foster. Shops allow us to appreciate architecture up close, to see and handle details and materials, and to participate in a highly choreographed spatial experience first-hand. It's condensed architecture, with added graphics and bespoke furniture, designed to make an immediate impact on us and affect our mood and actions.

One clear message from this kaleidoscopic survey of some of the best and most fascinating shops of the twentieth century, is that today's rapid evolution and transformation of the high street is far from unprecedented. In many cases, we are featuring not free-standing new buildings, but design-led fit-outs, intended as little more than transient stage sets. Some major works by leading architects had remarkably short lives. For instance, Denys Lasdun's Peter Robinson on The Strand opened in 1959 and was demolished in 1996, none of Wells Coates' work for Cryséde or Cresta survives, nor that of Patrick Gwynne for Freeman Hardy & Willis. The fact that Burton menswear stores often had billiard halls upstairs has been largely forgotten, as has the provision of lending libraries in branches of Boots, although both were deeply embedded in our culture – for instance in the film *Brief Encounter*, the heroine Laura's weekly routine includes a regular trip to Boots to change her books and the practice was top of John Betjeman's ironic list of 'what our Nation stands for' in his 1940 poem 'In Westminster Abbey'.

Will automated tills and more sophisticated methods of scanning and billing continue to automate the shopping experience? Or will we return to more intimate and

LEFT Denys Lasdun's Peter Robinson, The Strand, London, 1959, demolished 1996

personal encounters in terms of both buildings and personnel? All of the examples brought together here show that shops have long been designed to do more than just facilitate the exchanging of goods. In researching her entry on the Croydon IKEA (page 226) Katrina Navickas found that a somewhat cynical blogger had compared a trip to IKEA to an outing to another converted power station: 'It's very similar to a trip to Tate Modern (3.6 million visitors per year). Looking. Shuffling. Self-awareness. Hunger. Flirting. Looking. Imagining. Not quite enjoying. Smugness. Not quite understanding.' Perhaps that quote gives some clue as to where we have gone wrong, and what we need to challenge. If they are to survive, our shops need to support us having more fun, and more social interaction, and to use design to make that happen.

Catherine Croft
c20society.org.uk

RIGHT Freeman, Hardy & Willis, Catford, south London by Patrick Gwynne, 1953, remodelled as a Curtess shoe shop in 1955

11

1916 –
1929

Burdon House

Location: 1–4 Burdon Road, Sunderland
Designed by: William Bell and Arthur Pollard, North Eastern Railway Architect's Department
Opened: 1916
Listed: Grade II

The North Eastern Railway, responsible for lines from York into the Scottish Borders, had a reputation for innovation, sound economics and good design. Hence the building of prestigious shops to support offices for its staff in the heart of the city centre; the railway runs directly behind. It was also the first railway company to appoint a full-time salaried architect, in 1854, with William Bell occupying the post from 1877 to 1914. He adopted Queen Anne and classical styles, continued by his successor Arthur Pollard.

Designed in 1914, the style of Burdon House was classical, executed in local ashlar with giant pilasters. Perhaps it was ownership by the railway that allowed the scheme to be completed in wartime. The shopfronts survive unusually well, with a double row of small top lights over the main shopfront, in rusticated surrounds. The bowed corner unit has long been a bar, while student accommodation now occupies the other floors.

Elain Harwood

14

Heal's

Location: Tottenham Court Road, London
Designed by: Cecil Brewer, in
partnership with A. Dunbar Smith
Opened: 1916
Listed: Grade II*

Ambrose Heal transformed his family's bed-manufacturing business into makers and retailers of Arts and Crafts furnishings of a wholesome, high-minded kind. Rebuilding premises at 196 Tottenham Court Road, he employed his cousin, Cecil Brewer, with A. Dunbar Smith, in 1912–16, the latter the date on the building. Heal and Brewer visited the Deutsche Werkbund exhibition in Cologne in 1914, and the latter confessed himself 'all agog with German things afloat in my head'. The steel-framed, stone-clad façade completed under wartime conditions, is an early example of 'stripped classicism' with decorative panels by Joseph Armitage. It set a standard for structural clarity and decorative restraint. The recessed arcade with projecting blinds on special bronze brackets is a notable feature. The shop was extended to the south by five bays in 1936–8 by Edward Maufe, whose wife Prudence worked for Heal's, and to the north in 1961–2 by Fitzroy Robinson & Partners in a modern yet respectful idiom.

Alan Powers

HOUSE OF FRASER

HOUSE OF FRASER

HOUSE OF FRASER

RODDIS

CLOSING DOWN
20% OFF

CLOSING DOWN
20% OFF

CLOSING DOWN
20% OFF

CLOSING DOWN
20% OFF
7 DAYS TO GO

Brights, later House of Fraser

Location: Old Christchurch Road, Bournemouth
Designed by: Reynolds and Tomlins (attributed)
Opened: c.1920
Listed: Grade II

Brights Stores was founded by Frederick Bright in 1871 in The Arcade, next door to its current building in Old Christchurch Road. Around 1905, Brights enlarged their store with an innovative new iron-framed extension, accommodating shops and showrooms with a restaurant and offices above. A decade or so later, the store, then Bright and Colston, was upgraded and its nineteenth-century north and east elevations remodelled in fashionable Art Deco style. This work has been attributed to the Bournemouth-based architects who designed the streamlined Dolcis store on the corner about 15 years later. The Old Christchurch Road elevation is clad in cream tiles, supplied by Carter and Co. of Poole, forming pilasters and arches which frame the windows and define the bays, while terracotta panels, decorated with sunbursts in blue and brown faience, express the floors of the steel-framed structure behind. Early twentieth-century staircases, cast-iron columns and decorative plasterwork survive inside.

Coco Whitaker

Piccadilly Chambers

Location: 1, 3 and 5 Piccadilly, York
Designed by: Walter Brierley with James Rutherford
Opened: 1921
Listed: Grade II

Walter Brierley, nicknamed the Lutyens of the North, designed over 300 buildings across Yorkshire and beyond throughout his 40-year career at the turn of the century. The profound impact that his prolific output had on the built fabric of York has cemented Brierley as a quintessential author of the city, bringing Wrenaissance and later neo-Georgian design to its historic streetscape.

Piccadilly Chambers was one of Brierley's last works and sits at the south end of Parliament Street, the city's main market until 1955. The building – a bank and offices originally including shops – is firmly neo-Georgian, of warm red brick above a chaste ground floor of local stone. However, it features a delightful angled corner wholly of ashlar with giant Corinthian pilasters across the upper floors. Though opened in 1921, the rainwater heads are dated 1915, a clear example of delays caused by the First World War.

Finn Walsh

Former Woolworths, Preston

Location: 30–31 Fishergate, Preston
Designed by: William Priddle
Opened: 1923

Frank Woolworth opened his first store in America in 1879. The first British store opened in Liverpool in 1909, followed in 1910 by a second in Fishergate, Preston. This relocated to its current site in 1923, trading until the collapse of Woolworths in 2008.

Woolworths quickly developed a distinctive, albeit largely traditional style for their shops and employed their own architects, William Priddle serving from 1919 or earlier until his death in 1932. Like Burton, Woolworths used Priddle and his assistants to brand an expanding chain. His elaborate white faience frontage has eight two-storey columns topped by vaguely Egyptian Moderne capital decorations: 1922 was the year Tutankhamun's tomb was discovered, but the motifs were used into the 1930s. The central vertical panel has a tall oriel window. White faience, probably by Shaws of Darwen, was a practical self-cleaning surface for Preston's rainy, sooty weather. The building now houses a branch of Next.

Aidan Turner-Bishop

Kennedy's Sausages

Location: 305 Walworth Road, London
Opened: c.1923
Listed: Grade II

Kennedy's sold sausages for cooking at home, and pies for consumption straight away. When the firm ceased trading in 2007 after nearly 140 years, the Twentieth Century Society put all their surviving premises across south London forward for listing. This branch is one of several with an original timber shopfront and grey granite stallriser, and four stained glass transom lights in an Art Deco sunburst design. The distinctive fascia is of polished glass and has a makers' mark reading 'W. Piggot Ltd (brilliant process)'; letters of V-section were impressed into copper sheets with steel dies and then covered in glass.

The interior is clad in coloured tiles, green beneath the timber dado rail and primrose yellow up to the picture rail, and some original fittings remain. Since listing, several businesses have occupied the site, but it is currently empty. We hope that newly available grant funding will make proper restoration feasible.

Catherine Croft

Reliance Arcade, Market Row and Granville Arcade

Location: Brixton, London
Designed by: R. S. Andrews and
J. Peascod (Market Row); Alfred and
Vincent Burr (Granville Arcade, now
Brixton Village)
Opened: 1925–37
Listed: Grade II

These three market buildings thread through the centre of Brixton, crowded with small shops and stalls. They were twice proposed for total demolition, in the 1960s and again in the early 2000s, when the Twentieth Century Society applied for listing.

The subsequent list description notes the significance of the Egyptian frontage inspired by the discovery of Tutankhamen's tomb in 1922, interiors featuring black vitrolite, and use of both concrete and steel truss roof structures to let in plenty of light, but the application was initially turned down. Only after a campaign backed by the local MP emphasised the historic significance of the markets to the Afro-Caribbean community was the complex listed: 'The successful adoption of the markets is the clearest architectural manifestation of the major wave of immigration that had such an important impact on the cultural and social landscape of post-war Britain, and is thus a site with considerable historical resonance.'

Catherine Croft

Vigo House, Empire House, Westmorland House and New Gallery

Location: 115–131 Regent Street, London
Designed by: Sir John Burnet and Partners
Opened: 1925
Listed: Grade II

The rebuilding of John Nash's Regent Street by the Crown Estates, mainly carried out in the 1920s, was widely condemned for its poor taste, but the block on the west side just north of the Quadrant, incorporating the New Gallery as a cinema, designed in 1920–25, has usually been judged a success. Commissioned by a former Edinburgh patron, R. W. Forsyth, proprietor of a successful menswear business, John Burnet relied increasingly on Thomas Tait, who was able to modulate the classicism of his senior partner towards plainer forms. *The Times* grouped it among designs showing 'steady progress in designing for masonry and brickwork in well-proportioned masses, instead of relying on the trimmings of style', while for Howard Robertson, the block had 'one of the finest fronts in Regent Street', although he was less happy with the curved corners and their heavy domes. Sculpture was contributed by Sir William Reid Dick.

Alan Powers

Liberty's

Location: Regent Street and Great Marlborough Street, London
Designed by: Edwin T. Hall and E. Stanley Hall
Opened: 1926
Listed: Grade II

Designed in 1914 but held back for over ten years, Edwin T. Hall and his son, E. Stanley Hall, produced an unusual Portland stone façade on Regent Street with a concave upper story bearing a narrative frieze and stone figures appearing to look over the parapet. For the larger, side-street block they had greater freedom. Within its original shop, Liberty's (founded in 1875) had already adopted a 'Tudor feeling' and the early 1920s marked a high point of enthusiasm for this look. 'The Tudor period is the most genuinely English period' wrote Ivor Stewart-Liberty in 1924, on completion of his half-timbered shop commissioned from the same architects. Oak from old warships reaffirmed the nostalgia and provided a dark background for displaying the company's famous fabrics. A jumbled rather than unified street view disguised the successful modern business. The company is still trading under the original name in the Tudor building.

Alan Powers

MARKETS, ARCADES, PRECINCTS AND SHOPPING CENTRES

Markets date back to Roman times, controlled by royal charters from the Middle Ages. These were street markets, and it was only in the seventeenth century that some form of cover was introduced, initially for fish and meat. Substantial indoor markets date only from the nineteenth century. Some towns erected specialist retail markets for foodstuffs and dry goods, though most separated only meat and fish – the most essential for reasons of hygiene and smell. Sheffield's historic castle area saw the development of fish and meat markets (rebuilt in 1928–30), the dry goods Norfolk Market, the Castlefolds wholesale market and the open-air Sheaf Market, a flea market held on Tuesdays and Saturdays – every level of small trader was thus catered for within a small area. Nottingham's historic open-air market was swept out of the Market Square into new covered markets opened in 1928 on a slum clearance site in Huntingdon Street, leaving the old square to be reconfigured as a formal setting for the new Council House. In another project that also involved slum clearance, the Corporation of the City of London took over Spitalfields Market in 1920 and doubled its extent by 1928. Though the 1897 buildings survive, those of the 1920s have been demolished, a pattern seen across the country.

Markets assumed a symbolic importance in the war, for they continued trading after conventional shops had been bombed out and provided a lifeline for local economies;

even Marks & Spencer took a market stall after Plymouth city centre was destroyed. In consequence they assumed an important position economically and as architectural features when bomb-damaged cities came to be rebuilt. In other towns and cities, the large, prime sites occupied by market buildings made them targets for redevelopment as part of new shopping precincts. New markets provided architectural drama in new town centres at Hartlepool and Huddersfield, unlike at Nottingham, where the replacement for the Central Market was a nondescript adjunct to the Victoria Centre opened in 1972. The best post-war markets were virtuoso pieces of engineering, and survivals include arched concrete shells at Plymouth (1959), umbrella-like shells at Huddersfield (1968–70), cantilevered 'gull-wing' roofs at Bury, built in 1968–71, and cranked cantilevers at Hartlepool (1967–71). The markets at Plymouth, Coventry and Huddersfield are listed, but others of equal bravado have been destroyed, as at Sheffield, Blackburn and Accrington. Only Swansea Market, opened in 1961, made a feature of an arched steel roof, a token of support for local industry. All had to combine a broad span, only Huddersfield having columns, with large areas of glazing to bring natural light to the heart of these enclosed buildings, all set in the centre of an urban block surrounded by small shops and cafés.

Similar lighting problems on a smaller scale faced the builders of shopping arcades, single malls of specialist luxury

RIGHT Queensgate Market, Huddersfield, J Seymour Harris Partnership, 1968–70

shops that created specialist retail space while also linking two or more major shopping streets. They grew out of colonnaded shopping pavements and exchanges, and first appeared in Paris. The first in Britain was the Royal Opera Arcade, in London, opened in 1821. Arcades assumed a civic grandeur when the concept was translated to Italy, and the Galleria Vittorio Emanuele II built in Milan between 1865 and 1877 inspired buildings as diverse as the Letchworth Arcade of 1922 (after Ebenezer Howard included a shopping galleria or 'Crystal Palace' in his vision of a garden city), Exchange Buildings of 1924–9 in Nottingham and Milton Keynes Shopping Building of 1975–9.

More arcades were built in the interwar period than has hitherto been recognised, and details often survive well, such as glazed roofs and terrazzo floorings; covenants and leasehold terms ensure a high survival rate even for shopfronts. The Harris Arcade of 1929–31 in Reading, incorporating an earlier motor showroom, has shop fronts of metal and timber painted to resemble bronze with Art Deco details. A more rough-shod but colourful complex survives at Brixton, south London, where the Reliance Arcade of 1925, Market Row of 1928 and the former Granville Arcade of 1937 were threaded through and behind existing buildings. From its origins as a working-class market, Brixton Market became the centre of small businesses for the local Black community and is being repurposed again for street food sellers. These examples are among only a handful of interwar arcades to be listed.

Arcades were historically roofed, private, gated and secure, ideal for displaying small, valuable goods such as silks and jewellery. When in 1906 the Bedford Estate applied to build Sicilian Avenue as a pedestrian street open to the air, the London County Council had to rapidly reinterpret the conditions of the London Building Acts to allow the scheme, completed in 1910. A pedestrian thoroughfare lined with small specialist shops offering a picturesque walk to Exeter Cathedral, named Princesshay after the future Queen Elizabeth visited the city, was a key feature of Thomas Sharp's plan for rebuilding the city following the Second World War. It was substantially realised in the late-1950s but was demolished in 2005–7.

As car ownership grew, so the separation of vehicles and pedestrians became increasingly important to the safety and comfort of shoppers. In the United States, shopping centres became features of wartime settlements connected with the munitions industry. In Britain, the assistant commissioner of the Metropolitan Police, Alker Tripp, advocated shopping precincts for pedestrian safety, while in Amsterdam the sixteenth century Kalverstraat was closed to traffic as early as 1924. Donald Gibson, Coventry's city architect, saw how traffic moved more freely round the central area following the closure of its principal shopping street by

RIGHT Exchange Buildings, Nottingham, T. Cecil Howitt, 1926–9

war damage and so redesigned it as a pedestrian precinct as early as 1941, though not the first to be built. A pioneering built model was provided by Rotterdam's Lijnbaan, a new pedestrian shopping street built in 1952–3 to the designs of Johannes van den Broek and Jacob Bakema, which has in turn become a model example of restoration following its heritage designation in 2010. In the early 1950s it was visited by Coventry councillors, and by representatives of Stevenage Development Corporation ahead of the building of their own precinct, Queensway, lined with shops to an exceptionally unified design inspired by an initial scheme from no less than Clarence Stein, at the time perhaps America's leading planner. In the United States, Morris Ketchum designed Shoppers' World in Framingham near Boston in 1951 as a suburban mall anchored by a department store at each end to encourage footfall right through the site, surrounded by car parking; though not the first, it was the first American precinct to be widely published and imitated. Here was the start of the shopping centre as a leisure destination, rather than as a resource for life's essentials.

A subsequent American development was of still more lasting significance. Victor Gruen (born Viktor Grünbaum) was a Viennese refugee who specialised in retail buildings and later shopping centres, building outdoor malls in California and the Midwest, before hitting on the idea of enclosed ones. He designed America's first fully indoor,

climate-controlled shopping centre opened in 1956 at Edina, Minnesota, a suburb of Minneapolis St Paul, although Ralph Erskine's small 'Shopping' building at Luleå in northern Sweden opened slightly earlier, in 1955. The concept had obvious advantages for cold climates and was made possible by the arrival of efficient fluorescent lighting after the Second World War. In Britain the first indoor shopping centres were at the Elephant and Castle in south London, built in 1962–5 to the designs of a husband-and-wife team, Paul Boissevain and Barbara Osmond, and the Bull Ring in Birmingham, built in 1961-4 by Sydney Greenwood, in-house architect for the builders John Laing & Son, who visited America before completing his design. Both followed competitions for teams of architects and developers working together, held in 1959–60, and both have been demolished.

Wandsworth was unusual among the inner London boroughs in building its own shopping centre and flats in harness with a speculative developer, Sam Chippindale, in 1971. More malls appeared in the market towns absorbed into Greater London from 1965. These included the Whitgift Centre in Croydon in 1968–70 (since rebuilt) and indoor malls followed at Stratford (1973) and Eden Walk, Kingston (1979). A far larger centre opened at Brent Cross in 1972–6, innovative at the time for being a destination in its own right – set close to a motorway – rather than part of a traditional town centre or new town suburb. Otherwise,

the high land values and London's unique structure of local government has ensured that the traditional high street has held up better than elsewhere.

Elsewhere, many local authorities saw investment in their town centres as a means of increasing income from business rates, especially where they had a freehold such as a wholesale market or abattoir to redevelop. A new centre was also the best way to regenerate their towns and cities, and particularly to bring something of Swinging London through chain stores and discotheques to the Midlands and the North. A few authorities took on the redevelopment themselves. Newcastle's shops had the highest turnover in the country and T. Dan Smith, leader of the council from 1959–65, argued that as the corporation owned most of the land, redevelopment would be painless and profitable so long as it financed the scheme itself. His schemes included an open shopping precinct and library by Sir Basil Spence, Glover & Ferguson, and a project to rebuild Eldon Square with shops and a hotel by Arne Jacobsen.

However, most authorities leased these prime sites to developers such as Chippindale, Ravenseft and Murrayfield (the latter with strong links to the Labour Party), who could invest larger sums and attract the major multiples. Of these the most notable was Sam Chippindale, a Yorkshire estate agent, who had specialised in finding sites for chain stores such as Marks & Spencer before forming the Arndale

LEFT The Bull Ring, Birmingham, Sydney Greenwood, in-house architect for John Laing & Son, 1961–4

Property Company in 1951 with a local investor, Arnold Hagenbach. They progressed from small shopping parades to the building of large open-air precincts at Jarrow, Shipley and elsewhere in the North. But when, in 1960, Chippindale visited Australia, he became convinced that indoor centres were the future. The success of his Arndale Centres was based on his knowledge of footfall in Britain's high streets and a skill in attracting the major multiples to take anchor sites, beginning at Cross Gates, Leeds, opened in 1967. Chippindale built only 16 indoor shopping centres, but he set a trend that was followed across Great Britain, where 488 centres were built between 1965 and 1983.

Some towns remodelled their town centres several times over: St Peter's Shopping Centre, Oldham, designed by Richard Seifert & Partners and opened in 1967, was largely superseded by an indoor extension in 1981 and replaced by the Spindles Centre in 1992, which is itself up for redevelopment as of 2022. At Birmingham, the Bull Ring has been replaced by a more piecemeal shopping centre, restoring an open street, and a similar scheme was approved for Nottingham, though in 2022 it is set to be superseded by a mix of shops, residential development and a new library. A shopping centre could always support other town centre investment: the Eagle Centre (now Intu) built at Derby in 1970–5 included not only a new covered market but also a theatre, designed by Roderick Ham. Now the Eagle Market

is set to close in turn, thanks to a reduced footfall and investment elsewhere; the rise of 'pop-up' venues for small traders seems to be at the expense of permanent, architect-designed spaces. And while there is some hope for surviving interwar markets and arcades, the demolition of those from the 1960s and 1970s looks set to continue, as at Bradford, where the Oastler and Kirkgate markets – along with the indoor Kirkgate Centre – will be replaced by a single hall and food mall in Darley Street. Such moves also mark a change from public to private spaces, epitomised by the Milton Keynes Shopping Building – once open 24 hours a day but now privatised and with strict opening hours.

The private mall reached its apogee when planners began to allow out-of-town malls on American lines in the 1980s. They were encouraged to bring jobs and investment to areas with social and economic problems, walled towns built at the expense of the traditional high street, with car parking and access to motorways essential, and food courts and cinemas offering all-day entertainment alongside the shops. Bluewater, the regeneration of a chalk quarry in 1999, and the Trafford Centre – classical excess with palm trees built in 1998 to designs by Rodney Carran of Chapman Taylor – show how far we have come from the humble produce market.

Elain Harwood

RIGHT Queensway, Stevenage, Leonard Vincent, Stevenage Development Corporation, 1956–9

Griffin & Spalding, later Debenhams

Location: Long Row, Nottingham
Designed by: Bromley and Watkins (additions)
Opened: 1927
Listed: Grade II

Griffin & Spalding was Nottingham's largest and most prominent department store, evolving from Dickinson's drapery of 1846. The firm first commissioned rock-faced buildings on the new Market Street cut through in 1865. It then rebuilt the prominent corner site it had been thus gifted, the eastern third in 1919–20 and the centrepiece and corner in 1927. Albert Nelson Bromley (1850–1934) was then Nottingham's leading architect, having earlier designed mock-Tudor stores for Jesse Boot across Britain. Here, however, the chosen style was authoritatively neo-classical above the traditional ground-floor colonnade and executed in dignified Portland stone, among its first uses in the city. The store continued to expand, rebuilding No. 36 Long Row in the late 1950s. Inside, the store was labyrinthine, a maze of low ceilings and short staircases making an odd contrast to the luxuriousness of the goods on offer. The store closed in May 2021 and is looking for a reuse.

Elain Harwood

W. H. Smith, Winchester

Location: 110 High Street, Winchester
Designed by: J. W. Williamson
Opened: 1927
Listed: Grade II

W. H. Smith came to prominence running railway station bookstalls, until in 1905 the company lost 250 contracts following a rent hike. It turned to shops, appointing the architect Frank C. Bayliss as its shopfitter. For new buildings, Bayliss favoured neo-Tudor styles, fashionable for bookshops in the nineteenth century, but allowed variations to suit individual settings and commissioned local architects, such as Blount and Williamson of Salisbury. Thus, the Winchester store resembles a medieval hall, though its dated rainwater heads feature sailing ships. Bayliss determined the standard low Cotswold stone risers, oak-framed shop fronts and bullseye glass to the upper windowpanes. Inside, part of the ground floor was a lending library, while the first-floor showroom with its hammerbeam roof was originally a tearoom, entered from Parchment Street to the side. Painted moulded plasterwork and murals depict local and international scenes from history, those in the end gables inevitably featuring King Arthur.

Elain Harwood

The Exchange

Location: High Street, Nottingham
Designed by: T. Cecil Howitt
Opened: 1929
Listed: Grade II*

Nottingham's Council House replaced an Exchange Hall of 1724–6, remodelled in 1814–15. T. Cecil Howitt, the city housing architect, expected that the nearby University College would accommodate most of the urgently needed council offices, so proposed rebuilding the Exchange as a superior shopping arcade, modelled on Milan's Galleria Vittorio Emanuele II. Three top-lit arcades, incorporating an existing bank and insurance offices, meet under a dome modelled on St Paul's Cathedral. In its spandrels, local artists Noel Denholm Davis and Frederick Hammersley Ball painted scenes featuring historic visits from rampaging Danes, William I, Robin Hood and Charles I in vivid Eastman colour. Howitt appears as William I's surveyor, while Little John was modelled on Notts County's goalkeeper Albert Iremonger. The shops survive so completely because until 1983 they were almost all occupied by a single upmarket grocer, Burtons. In turn, income from the arcade has contributed to the preservation of the council suite in the west wing.

Elain Harwood

1930 –
1949

O. & C. Butcher

Location: 121–131 High Street, Aldeburgh, Suffolk
Opened: Shopfront early 1930s

Edward Butcher's Supply Stores opened on the edge of Aldeburgh in 1884, the year that the golf course was founded, bringing a new kind of holiday visitor. The next generation, Owen and Clifford, moved the business to their present site and it became a men's and women's outfitters and shoe shop. The present 1930s shopfront is a rare survival of a 'draper's arcade'. The deep recess and island display showcase suited the retail strategy of crowding the windows with goods. The sacrifice of shop floor area was justified by enabling customers to linger and do their window shopping in a sheltered spot. The floor was usually a form of mosaic, here with a simple green outline. The leaded-light upper windows with their Art Deco fountain design are a delightful period feature. In 2007 the business was bought by James Stacey, whose family ran a similar shop for many years in Harleston, Norfolk.

Alan Powers

SHOE DEPARTMENT

INFORMATION

James Howell & Co.

Location: St Mary Street, Cardiff
Designed by: Ivor Jones and
Percy Thomas
Opened: 1930
Listed: Grade II*

This former department store occupies over half of the city block south of Cardiff's indoor market and faces three streets. Much of the St Mary Street frontage is late Victorian but at the Wharton Street corner is a mini-Selfridges – a Percy Thomas-designed, North-American-Beaux-Arts-inspired pavilion block in Portland stone. Monumental in scale with giant Ionic columns to the three bays to St Mary Street, the corner is rounded into Wharton Street where a Doric pilaster order takes over. At ground floor level, the shopfronts are framed in bronze with integral store nameplates to the plinths. It is a fine example of interwar classicism by Wales's pre-eminent twentieth-century architect and won a RIBA Bronze Medal in 1930. Continuing along Wharton Street is a 1930s simplified classical block, also by Thomas, leading at the other end to a post-war, international modern building that, with its three continuous bands of windows, curves dramatically around the corner to Trinity Street.

Jonathan Vining

Boots the Chemist, Bexhill-on-Sea

Location: 14–16 Devonshire Road, Bexhill-on-Sea, East Sussex
Designed by: Percy J. Bartlett
Opened: c.1931

Bexhill-on-Sea was all astir when Boots the Chemist replaced a pair of conventional Victorian terraced houses – one of them home to the company's local branch since 1913 – with a sleek white building. The flat roof and strong horizontal lines of 'Bexhill's prison' or 'Noah's Ark' appeared starkly modern.

Boots enjoyed a reputation for designing stores to suit their context, often including local references. When Percy J. Bartlett of Nottingham took over as company architect in 1927, the favoured approach was neo-Georgian. The streamline moderne style chosen for Bexhill was, consequently, a novel departure. This architectural fashion was adopted around the same time by F. W. Woolworth in nearby Worthing, and swiftly became associated with the seaside.

After Bexhill's De La Warr Pavilion opened in 1935, Boots declared that it was merely following their lead, claiming: 'Boots the Chemist forestalled the city fathers in visualising Bexhill of the future'.

Kathryn A. Morrison

The Headrow

Location: Leeds
Designed by: Sir Reginald Blomfield (lead architect)
Opened: 1931 onwards
Listed: Grade II

Visiting in c.1934, John Betjeman dismissed The Headrow as 'depressing' and Nikolaus Pevsner later considered it 'tame', but the showcase high street has defied such criticism. A project launched in the mid-1920s had seen supervision of the modelling of the narrow, historic thoroughfare entrusted to Reginald Blomfield, who had worked on the reconstruction of London's Regent Street.

Blomfield designed Permanent House and the contiguous Headrow buildings, a development completed in 1931 and setting a grand classical model for the reconstruction or refronting of the entire street with shops, offices, a cinema and banks. He was also responsible for a monumental bank at the corner of Vicar Lane, though his designs for Lewis's department store were only partially realised, the simpler upper storeys being added in the 1950s. A classical filling station – which once addressed the monumentally modernist Quarry Hill Flats – was Blomfield's final contribution, with other buildings assigned to lesser hands.

Kenneth Powell

Burton Menswear, Halifax

Location: Borough Market, Halifax
Designed by: Harry Wilson
Opened: 1931–2

West Yorkshire was the heart of Sir Montague Burton's empire, and his Halifax store runs a close second to Charles Barry's heroic town hall in the town centre. Company architect Harry Wilson's stock-in-trade stone-clad classicism was here enlivened with Art Deco chevron-patterned spandrel panels and no fewer than 20 elephant head capitals, mounted above paired ribbed pilasters. High on the front elevation was the unmissable legend 'BURTON Buildings'. It benefitted from a prime corner site, as favoured by Burton's in-house property arm. There was no clear explanation for the frequently used elephant head motif. Wilson had previously worked for Woolworths, who favoured lions, seemingly to emphasise their allegiance to Britain. Burton's clothing factory on Hudson Road, Leeds, was the biggest in the world and this store, its upper floors for office use with space for a billiard hall (Burton was a committed teetotaller), was an inescapably bold statement. Now it is a McDonald's.

Gillian Darley

India Buildings

Location: Water Street, Liverpool
Designed by: Herbert Rowse with
Arnold Thornley
Opened: 1932
Listed: Grade II*

India Buildings was built for Alfred Holt of the Blue Funnel Line shipping company over two city blocks, absorbing a whole street and replacing offices built for his grandfather, George Holt, in the 1830s. Herbert Rowse had seen, in Canada and the United States, the architecture that so inspired his tutor at the Liverpool School of Architecture, Sir Charles Reilly. In the hands of Reilly's students, this was translated into a monumental neo-classicism known as the 'Liverpool manner' and India Buildings is a fine example. A late addition to the design was a noble, tunnel-vaulted arcade of shops running right through the building and roughly following the line of the lost street. Detailed in bronze with lighting by the Bromsgrove Guild, the arcade sadly closed to the public in 2017 as part of a major refurbishment for HMRC, though the individual units live on as small meeting rooms.

Andrew Jackson

Sussex Street

Location: between Sidney and Hobson streets, Cambridge
Designed by: E. R. Barrow
Opened: 1932, 1939
Listed: Grade II

Sussex Street existed by 1690, and may be medieval, but it was entirely rebuilt by Sidney Sussex College in 1928–39. Barrow rebuilt the south side first, in a simple early Georgian style using dark red brick with yellow stone detailing. An arcade shelters bronze framed shopfronts behind and college accommodation above, with some offices, rising to four storeys at the ends. Whereas this side takes the form of a shallow crescent, when Barrow returned in 1938–9 to rebuild the north side he repeated the same idiom as a straight façade, lined with stone piers. The buildings are named after college dignitaries. A 'bridge of sighs' in similar brickwork was added by Pleasance, Hookham & Nix for the college in 1991. The street was then pedestrianised, an oasis of calm and a complete piece of townscape, rightly considered by Nikolaus Pevsner to be 'the best piece of pre-war urban planning at Cambridge'.

Elain Harwood

Blunts Shoes

Location: 128–132 Granby Street, Leicester
Designed by: Symington, Prince and Pike
Opened: 1933
Listed: Grade II

This unusually elaborate Art Deco shop front is a prominent landmark on what was appropriately known in the 1930s as Granby Corner, the entrance to Leicester's principal shopping street. It was designed for local furniture manufacturer Nathan Harris and built of fine Portland stone. The three blocks of windows wrapped around the corner are articulated by giant fluted pilasters, their capitals featuring Ionic scrolls. The attic is set back, with contrasting horizontal bands under a green tiled roof and a central flagpole. To the left a taller range features continuous banks of glazing through three storeys. The ground floor is similar all round and has alternating large windows with shaped heads and smaller shop fronts and doors with decorative overlights, now with green striped blinds to match the green metal window surrounds. Other Art Deco details include the tiled entrance step and surrounds to the glass bricks which light the basement.

Elain Harwood

Derry & Toms and Barkers

Location: Kensington
High Street, London
Designed by: Bernard George
Opened: 1933, 1938 respectively
Listed: Grade II* and II

Three great department stores followed the arrival of Kensington High Street Station in 1867, first Derry & Toms, then Barkers and Pontings. By 1920 John Barker & Co. owned all three, and in 1928 acquired land to rebuild the two main stores. Derry & Toms was planned on the American 'horizontal' or open-plan system, advised by C. A. Wheeler of Chicago. Banks of lifts were faced in onyx and marble, with only modest escape stairs. The classical façade featured aluminium panels by Walter Gilbert and the Bromsgrove Guild, while C. H. Mabey produced bas reliefs depicting labour and technology. The roof garden was the largest in Europe. The store closed in 1973 but flowered briefly as Biba. Barkers' Art Deco store (now subdivided) by contrast emphasised the verticality of the stair towers. Cast reliefs included household goods obtainable in the store, a futuristic jet engine plane, airship and locomotive.

Elain Harwood

Marks & Spencer, Falmouth

Location: Market Street, Falmouth
Designed by: W. A. Lewis & Partners
Opened: 1933

Falmouth was the first Marks & Spencer store in Cornwall and was constructed by Bovis. An extension in the early 1960s greatly increased floor space. At ground level there are three protruding window display bays with pearl grey granite stall risers and bronze detailing. The recessed entrances consist of two sets of doors, since altered, with a mainly cream mosaic floor and fluted pillars within, now cladded. Above sat the classic illuminated 'Marks & Spencer' signage, now long gone. The second storey is dominated by ten Crittall W20 Corporate range windows separated by a central projecting curvilinear shaped clock and egg and dart cornicing above.

The store ceased trading in February 2019 and was purchased by Acorn Blue for conversion to retail and residential use. This was initially refused by Cornwall Council, but permission was granted on appeal in 2023. It is in a conservation area with prime water frontage at the rear.

Robert Dowden

Southgate
Shopping Parade

Location: Southgate
Underground Station, Enfield
Designed by: Charles Holden
Opened: 1933

Charles Holden's curving parade for Southgate Underground Station serves multiple purposes. It allows buses to circulate around the station, making it into the civic hub beloved of London Underground's managing director and design supremo Frank Pick, and offers shelter from the elements. It also contains shops and offices, providing convenience for passengers and revenue for the Underground.

The two-storey parade nestles around the circular station building. The Buckinghamshire brick structure fits into the suburban scene, with the curved glazed ends showcasing the north European modernism seen by Holden and Pick on a fact-finding tour in 1930. The exterior has bronze shop fronts and columns finished in mosaic tiling. There are also kiosks inside the station building featuring signs with prominent metal lettering.

Holden included similarly curving kiosks at stations like Turnpike Lane and Rayners Lane, but the Southgate shops are his most assured commercial design, mixing beauty and utility.

Joshua Abbott

Former Newcastle Co-operative Society Department Store

Location: Newgate Street, Newcastle upon Tyne
Designed by: Leonard Gray Ekins
Opened: 1934; extended 1959
Listed: Grade II

Newcastle had a distinguished history of co-operation and built a department store here in 1886. The Co-operative Wholesale Society's architects' department was based in Manchester but had a branch in the city, where L.G. Ekins established his career before working in London from 1916.

From 1925 Ekins was involved with plans to build this flagship store, a rival to new commercial enterprises in Northumberland Street begun in 1930. The 1886 store was demolished, its 1902 extension modernised, and a new corner, north tower and six-bay frontage were completed in 1932. Another nine bays, the south tower and three bays beyond were finished in 1934 (extended by three bays in 1959 adopting the same style). There are Art Deco, Egyptian and downright unusual elements: a neon-lit barometer, small figures hauling handrails in stairwells. The 1930s alterations concealed the 1902 store's tall, cast-iron arcade, which reappeared during conversion work in 2014–16 and is visible in the rear courtyard. The building now houses a Premier Inn.

Lynn Pearson

THE CO-OPERATIVE MOVEMENT AND ITS STORES

Critical to understanding the Co-operative Movement's architectural heritage is the fact that individual co-operative societies were independent self-governing bodies, free to make their own decisions when it came to premises. From small beginnings in 1844, by 1901 there were nearly 1,500 retail co-ops in England, with a total of around 1.5 million members. Co-ops initially used members' subscriptions to build or rent their stores, where members were encouraged to shop. A percentage of any trading surplus was returned to members in regular dividend payments, the famous 'divi'. The more you spent in the store, the more you got back.

At first societies were reluctant to 'waste' money on attractive shop fronts, but by the turn of the century, co-op committees were spending hours choosing architects and builders, considering plans, discussing space allocations and suchlike. Some co-ops employed their own architects, but more often societies developed long-term relationships with local architectural practices. Over 4,000 co-op stores were built in England by 1910, along with much co-op housing.

Co-op shopping transactions were rather more convoluted than in the private sector, where customers generally paid at a central cash desk. In co-op stores, both society and customer needed a record of the purchase for dividend purposes, and individual salespeople normally dealt with transactions at the counter. Of course, there was more to life than shopping. Societies spent considerable

RIGHT Tudoresque Co-operative store, Shrewsbury, Francis Harris, 1923

sums on libraries, reading rooms and educational facilities, often in the form of meeting halls in the central premises. These areas, and especially the later co-op cafés and dance halls, provided an important non-conformist, pro-temperance space for customers to escape the world of advertising and the public house.

With hundreds of local co-ops erecting stores, it is no surprise to find that the result was architectural diversity, tempered by a desire to fit into the townscape and, crucially, obtain good value for money. Architectural style was rarely a matter for discussion. Co-operative symbolism offered a unifying factor, with beehives and wheatsheaves carved into pediments or appearing in doorway mosaics. This architectural free-for-all was frowned upon by the Manchester-based Co-operative Wholesale Society (CWS), formed in 1863 to improve supplies to English and Welsh co-ops; the Scottish CWS was established in 1868. From the late 1890s the CWS also offered an architecture, interior design and shopfitting service. However, individual societies could choose whether or not to patronise the CWS, and many did not.

Between the wars, co-op membership grew spectacularly, topping six million by the late 1930s when one in thirty of all shops was co-operatively owned. By this time, the CWS had developed into one of Britain's biggest manufacturing groups, with 155 factories, as well as farms and dairies and 63,000 employees worldwide, while its Architects' Department (CWSAD) had succeeded in persuading a growing number of local societies to use its services. During the mid-1930s the CWSAD was responsible for about two-thirds of new store commissions, as well as an extensive programme of factory, office and warehouse building.

Interwar stores survive in a wide range of styles, although many interiors have been altered significantly. We have neo-Georgian in Rochester (1928, L. G. Ekins of the CWSAD), neo-classical in Ashington (1924, Harrison, Ash & Blythe), Egyptianate in Falkirk (1931, James Callander) and a huge Tudoresque pile in Shrewsbury (1923) by the CWSAD's first chief architect, Francis Harris. His successor William Johnson produced the distinctive Bradford store (1933–6) with its horizontal bands of glazing. Its floorspace was open, with stairs moved to the fringes and escalators – the first in a co-op store – whisking shoppers upward. Some of Johnson's most innovative designs were for CWS factories, but none survive.

Several excellent Art Deco (former) stores – or at least façades – remain from the 1930s. Worth seeking out are Newcastle upon Tyne's unusual central premises (mostly 1930–4, L. G. Ekins), the glamorous white faience façade of Lewisham (1932–3, Samuel Ackroyd), the cinema-like vertical fin of Nuneaton's pharmacy (1938, Norman

RIGHT Art Deco former co-op, Lewisham, south London, Samuel Ackroyd, 1932-3

Jepson) and the curvy lines of Doncaster (1938–40, Harry Johnson). Pontypool's Art Deco store (1937–8) features a contemporary rendition of the wheatsheaf motif, making a rare interwar appearance. The CWSAD disliked overt co-operative messaging and encouraged societies to weed out dilapidated old branches. There was never a standard co-op exterior, although many interwar single-storey 'bungalow' stores looked very similar. The CWS shopfitting service cornered 85 per cent of co-op business by 1939, so store interiors began to have a family resemblance, although tailored to each location.

Many outstanding interwar stores have been demolished, notably the purest example of co-op modernism, Sheffield and Ecclesall's branch 40 (1936, John Blackhurst) in the city's southern suburbs, all strong horizontals, plate glass, black Vitrolite and angular lettering. Also gone is the same society's central premises extension (1929–30, William Johnson) with its stunning neo-classical white ceramic façade. The pilaster capitals were 8ft (2.4m) high, stylised polychrome flower vases, and Johnson also squeezed in some Egyptianate decorative elements, giving the whole an almost post-modern feel. Did the private sector produce anything quite so exotic? Lost too are Johnson's Blackpool store (1935–8), with lavish Art Deco interiors, and Peckham's unique moderne store (1927–8, Percy Westwood).

Although the co-op had acquired a reputation for drabness by the late 1930s, following the Second World War co-ops managed to maintain their share of trade, and were early adopters of self-service, experimenting with the system as early as 1942. The first self-service stores opened in 1948: in London, Upton Park's co-op and Wood Green Marks & Spencer's food department opened in January, followed by Southsea co-op in March 1948 (although only Southsea has a commemorative plaque). Three years later there were over 600 self-service co-ops. Later, new-build stores became rather bland externally, but could be dazzling inside, with interior designers keen to experiment, often in the numerous restaurants, milk bars and coffee bars. Strong colours were all the rage, and murals became commonplace. The best of the new department stores were extremely stylish, for instance Sheffield's CWSAD-designed Castle House (1960–4).

External tile and mosaic murals appeared on co-op stores from the mid-1950s, after Hungarian émigré designer Gyula Bajó joined the CWSAD. The earlier of his two surviving murals is on the former Letchworth, Hitchin and District Co-operative Society's department store (1956–8), overlooking Stevenage's showpiece Town Square. Bajó's colourful ceramic-tiled mural incorporated Stevenage-related images into a composition symbolising 'the spirit and activities of the Co-operative Movement'.

LEFT Co-operative Emporium and Danum House, Doncaster, T H Johnson, 1938-40

The mural was listed Grade II in 2022. Bajó later worked with Endre Hevezi on a mosaic mural marking the entrance to Ipswich's modernised premises (1960–5, CWSAD). Although the site is to be redeveloped, the mosaic – an abstract representation of co-operation based around a female figure holding a wheatsheaf – is to be relocated.

Two further co-op store murals survive. Hull co-op's new central premises opened in 1965, following more than a decade of construction overseen by the CWSAD's E. Philip Andrew. He commissioned artist Alan Boyson to design a mural for the curved wall above the store's main entrance. Boyson's 66ft (20m) high *Three Ships* mural (listed Grade II in 2019) celebrates the city's fishing industry, its three stylised ships – their interlinked masts spelling the word Hull – sailing on an Italian glass mosaic sea. The store is to be demolished, but the mural will be retained and restored. The last remaining mural fronted Scunthorpe's pharmacy (1963, Derek W. Brown), the biggest co-op pharmacy in Britain when opened. Its abstract, pharmacy-themed mosaic mural was designed by shopfitters Harris & Sheldon in conjunction with Brown. A fire in 1967 appears to have left the mural undamaged, but currently (in 2023) with no legal protection.

Total co-op store numbers rose until the early 1960s, when there were around 28,000 in England alone, but many were small, old-fashioned branches. Co-op trade declined as competition from the private sector increased, and independent societies were reluctant to pool resources. Eventually, however, mergers and amalgamations did take place, with the CWS taking over many failing societies. The total store count plummeted to around 3,000 in 1985. Three years earlier the CWSAD had been disbanded, with the loss of all its records. Many town centre stores built with 1960s optimism were gone within a few decades. Darlington's (1961–5, CWSAD), with its strange fibreglass frontage, was demolished in 1986, while the vast, seven-storey Bristol department store (1959–62) met its end in 1988. The disappearance of major co-op stores from town centres was a precursor of the present spate of department store closures.

The Co-op Group, established 2001, took on CWS (and former SCWS) functions and stores. By 2019, co-op stores comprised about 2,500 run directly by the Co-op Group, plus around 1,100 belonging to still independent regional and local societies, like the East of England Co-op. Modern co-ops – mostly convenience stores – often occupy recently built premises even in areas where original co-op buildings are extant. Perhaps two to three thousand traditional former co-op stores remain in England alone, hidden in plain sight but often identifiable by decorative wheatsheaves and beehives.

Lynn Pearson

RIGHT Alan Boyson's Three Ships mural on the Hull Co-operative store, E Philip Andrew of CWSAD, 1965

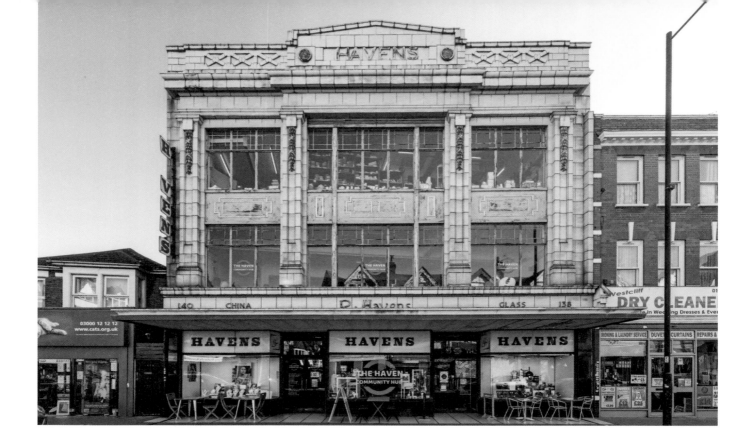

Havens

Location: 138–140 Hamlet Court
Road, Westcliff-on-Sea, Essex
Opened: 1935
Listed: Grade II

The family-owned department store is a dying breed on the high street.
Established in 1901 in this well-appointed extension of Southend-on-Sea, Havens
specialised in elegant household wares: china and glass as the storefront lettering
says. The Haven family bought the site in the 1920s, and their 'much-loved
building' opened in 1935. It is a confident Art Deco design, with a steel frame
clad in dusty beige Burmatofts faience, double staircases and decorative stained-
glass rooflights. The 2016 listing cites both the principal 1930s features and
1970s improvements, such as display windows, a canopy and back-lit signage.

As online shopping took over, the imaginative Haven brothers quickly
adapted, keeping limited stock on their top floor and partnering with Age
Concern Southend to run a Community Centre on the other two floors. The
centre is thriving, with activities, stalls and a café and there is a rehearsal space
upstairs. An exemplar for our times?

Gillian Darley

Former Mortimer Gall Electrical Company showroom

Location: 115 Cannon Street, London
Designed by: Walter Gropius and E. Maxwell Fry
Opened: 1936
Listed: Grade II (not shopfront)

Inserted at the base of a robust classical façade by J. L. Holmes of 1875, the black Vitrolite-faced shopfront of 1936 could have been by any number of designers or shopfitters. It is in fact the work of Walter Gropius, founder of the Bauhaus school in Germany in 1919, in partnership with E. Maxwell Fry, for the Mortimer Gall Electrical Goods Company. The stall riser is partly built of glass blocks to illuminate the basement, with slatted ventilation slots beneath the window glass. The deeply recessed entrance follows a bold curve, and the upper fascia originally contained the large-scale letters 'MG' in a thin sans-serif face. The shopfront served as a showcase for electrical appliances, many by German manufacturers. Gropius highlighted its non-loadbearing character by offsetting a supporting column away from the window. By the time it appeared in the *Architects' Journal* in 1937, he had emigrated to the United States.

Alan Powers

Simpsons, now Waterstones

Location: Piccadilly, London
Designed by: Joseph Emberton
with Felix Samuely, engineer
Opened: 1936
Listed: Grade II*

Selected by the Museum of Modern Art, New York, for the 1937 exhibition *Modern Architecture in England*, this upmarket outfitters set out to make an impression. Designed as the store 'for everything a man needs', a welded steel frame enabled five spacious shopping floors and a distinctive banded façade of horizontal fenestration and Portland stone cladding. After dark, concealed neon lighting illuminated this monochrome stylishness.

Joseph Emberton powerfully orchestrated the spatial and tactile. Concave non-reflecting display windows at street level, a cantilevered entrance canopy, and a travertine staircase with roughcast glass balustrading created an enveloping processional experience. Curved counters and luxurious surfaces unfolded sensuously. Oak and mahogany finishes represented quality, while Plymax and aluminium signalled the modern, as did the signage, displays and advertising of László Moholy-Nagy and Ashley Havinden.

Bookseller Waterstones bought the building in 1999 and it remains just possible to imagine the hush and bespoke glamour of the 1930s.

Catherine Moriarty

Sunwin House

Location: Sunbridge Road, Bradford
Designed by: W. A. Johnson
Opened: 1936
Listed: Grade II

The City of Bradford Co-operative Society's new Emporium on Sunbridge Road and Godwin Street brought architectural modernism to Bradford. Later its portmanteau address 'Sunwin' became a major Co-operative brand.

After becoming chief architect of the Co-operative Wholesale Society in 1924, W. A. Johnson's design was influenced by Erich Mendelsohn's 1928 Stuttgart Schocken Department Store. The steel-framed construction allows four storeys of deep horizontal bands of steel-framed glazing between bands of York stone facing. Two fully-glazed semi-circular turrets capped by curious square pavilions are bold. Their glamour matches the drama of the domes of the nearby 1914 Alhambra and 1930 New Victoria theatres. Much of the retail interior, a veneer-panelled boardroom and staircases with brass Art Deco handrails survive.

The Co-op sold up in 2005. The building stayed in retail use until 2011. In 2019 a £5,000 Architectural Heritage Fund project viability grant for a multi-use cultural hub was awarded, but the empty store was sold to a local investment company.

Christopher R. Marsden

Former Burton, Abergavenny

Location: 16–18 High Street, Abergavenny
Designed by: Nathaniel Martin (architect for Burton)
Opened: 1937
Listed: Grade II*

The distinctive moderne design of Burton stores, once in every British town, survives here virtually unaltered externally, elegantly fitted onto an awkward triangular site. Polished black granite fascias and bronze-framed windows give an air of tasteful luxury, the Burton ventilator grilles like the tailor's label in a bespoke suit. Above the display windows runs a 'chain of taste', linked lozenges containing the names of towns with stores. Curved windows form the narrow prow of the building and draw you into the deep central entrance. On Nevill Street a tile and terracotta panel exhorts, 'Let Montague Burton the Tailor of Taste Dress You'. The recessed upper floor, perhaps originally a billiard hall, became Chevron night club in 1975. Built in Portland stone, it has Crittall windows separated by fluted pilasters with the logo above. After Burton closed in 2017, the council enforced restoration of the building, now leased to Mountain Warehouse.

Susannah Charlton

W. S. Woods
Department Store

Location: 4–6 Station Road, Colwyn Bay
Designed by: Sidney Colwyn Foulkes
Opened: 1937
Listed: Grade II

By 1933, William Stead Wood, retailer of ladies' fashions, desired a department store with impact. He commissioned Sidney Colwyn Foulkes, a local architect renowned for using an eclectic range of architectural styles and elements for commercial and public buildings.

Foulkes was a master of both minimalist moderne and historical creativity, and here opted for an elegant Romanesque Revival. The upper façade is dominated by just two horizontal elements in the form of the corbel table and arcaded fenestration, the apparent simplicity from a distance belied by the beautiful intricacy and diversity of carved detailing to the ashlar Portland stone. Similar attention was given to a monogrammed lead planting trough, the stylised Art Deco busts to either end providing a surprising burst of modernity.

Despite listing in 1994, the original plate glass shop front with its advanced display case has been unsympathetically reordered with uPVC. Currently vacant and to let, its immediate future is uncertain.

Susan Fielding

Coronation Buildings

Location: Mansfield Road, Daybrook, Nottinghamshire
Designed by: Calvert, Jessop & Gleave
Opened: 1937
Listed: Grade II

Parades of shops, each offering a single product line or service, were important features of the housing estates built far from town centres in the 1930s. This example, commemorating George VI's coronation in May 1937, was built on the main road at Daybrook, then being linked to Nottingham by new housing in the streets behind and the Art Deco headquarters of the Home Brewery Co. (owners of the freeholds here). Calvert, Jessop & Gleave was a local practice responsible for many shops and offices in the city centre, mainly neo-Georgian in style. What is remarkable here is the survival of the upper windows, and particularly of the shop fronts with thin glazing bars giving a vertical accent to the main windows between the horizontal bands formed by the risers, opaque top-lights and fascias. The doorways are typically set back, to provide side windows for further display and a shelter on wet days.

Elain Harwood

Kingstone Store

Location: 65–67 Belgrave Gate, Leicester
Designed by: Raymond McGrath
Opened: 1937
Listed: Grade II

Sir Charles Keene, a leading businessman and Leicester councillor, was introduced to Raymond McGrath through Mansfield Forbes, the Cambridge don for whom McGrath had remodelled Finella as Cambridge's first modern movement house. Keene commissioned a furniture store, offices and a warehouse on the edge of Leicester city centre. A steel-framed building faced in concrete to the front and brick at the rear, the store is remarkable for its glass curtain walling on the upper floors over a simple canopy and shop front. It comprises bands of windows with pink Vitrolite fixed with copper cover strips. It is a true curtain wall, more adventurous for its date than the better-known Peter Jones in that its floor slabs are not exposed. McGrath published *Glass in Architecture and Decoration* in 1937, a pioneering work on the subject, and in 1939 went on to design a house for Keene, Land's End, now Carrygate, at nearby Galby.

Elain Harwood

Debenhams, Taunton

Location: North Street, Taunton
Designed by: George Baines & Son
Opened: 1938

This sleek, Art Deco department store was built for W. A. Chapman, a Taunton drapery firm established in 1864. Like many big retail stores, it developed organically: starting in a row of small nineteenth-century shops, and gradually taking over the neighbouring buildings, which were then either amalgamated or replaced. Chapman's expanded in 1938 and a new moderne frontage was created for 20–24 North Street by George Baines & Son with local builders W. Potter & Sons. Debenhams acquired W. A. Chapman in the early 1960s and extended the store again. The 1960s extension on North Street continues the 1930s Moderne elevation, extending its concrete canopy and brick upper levels and replicating its window design to provide continuity in the streetscape. The concrete glazed and clad north and rear elevations are more typical of the 1960s. Although the store was turned down for listing in January 2021, it was reprieved from the threat of demolition in 2023.

Coco Whitaker

Randalls
Department Store

Location: Vine Street, Uxbridge
Designed by: William L. Eves
Opened: 1938
Listed: Grade II

Furniture stores prospered as new houses multiplied across London's Metroland. They were aided by the arrival of hire purchase, whereby home builders could buy larger goods by weekly or monthly instalments, albeit at high interest rates. Randalls duly rebuilt their store of 1891 in a moderne style. It was long a rare, almost perfect survivor, designed by a local architect who built mainly for Uxbridge Urban District Council and in Buckinghamshire, but nevertheless secured wide reviews in the architectural press. It regularly appeared in television dramas.

William L. Eves's design owes much to Dutch modernist architect Willem Dudok, its long horizontals countered by a staircase tower, flagstaff, and – originally – a large clock. Doulton supplied the Carrara Ware faience, contrasted with red lettering that stood proud on a canopy infilled with glass lenses. Sir John Randall closed the family store in 2015. It has been redeveloped as flats with two retail/restaurant units that retain the original ground-floor shop fronts.

Elain Harwood

The Pantheon Marks & Spencer

Location: 163-173 Oxford Street, London
Designed by: Robert Lutyens and W. A. Lewis and Partners
Opened: 1938; extended early 1950s
Listed: Grade II

The chic styling of this store, which takes its name from James Wyatt's Pantheon of 1769–72 previously on the site, belies its highly practical façade system. The success of the high street chain in the 1920s and 1930s left it struggling to extend its shops without having to rebuild from scratch. In 1934 M&S turned to Robert Lutyens (only son of Sir Edwin) who devised a standardised, modular system on a 10ft (3m) grid, clad in artificial stone slabs, which could be applied to any frontage width and allowed for extensions at a later date; existing shops could also be refaced.

The Pantheon store was the only branch aside from Leeds (the origin of the chain) where artificial stone was abandoned in favour of highly polished black 'ebony' granite slabs. The shop front had a parade of island display cases, and the interior was richly appointed with walnut counters and wall panelling; sadly, now lost.

Posy Metz

Kendals, now House of Fraser

Location: 98–116 Deansgate, Manchester
Designed by: Office of J. S. Beaumont
Opened: 1939
Listed: Grade II

The work of the specialist store designer Louis Blanc, Kendals is a glamorous Portland stone cube with chamfered corners that fills an entire urban block. Quite unlike anything else in Manchester, its glass bricks in vertical stripes were probably the tallest windows in Britain until the modern era of frameless glass cladding. These bricks are slightly bowed in plan, draped like a fur coat, making a contrast to the straight edged stone with its Art Deco details.

Between 1919 and 1959, Kendal Milne & Co. was owned by Harrods. The new building was connected to the original Victorian store by a tunnel under Deansgate that became part of a web of pedestrian routes across the city avoiding cars and rain. Inside the store splayed escalators and big lifts shot customers to the top floor from where they could descend through quiet carpeted displays.

Andrew Crompton

Peter Jones

Location: Sloane Square, Chelsea, London
Designed by: William Crabtree, Charles Reilly, John Slater and Arthur Moberly
Opened: 1939
Listed: Grade II*

Bought by John Lewis in 1905, the Peter Jones department store on Sloane Square was reconstructed by their architectural advisor Charles Reilly, with recent graduate William Crabtree, who worked alongside the shop specialists, Slater & Moberly. 'Reilly did the talking on our side and I produced the drawings,' Crabtree explained, 'and I think we persuaded Slater and Moberly we were not such crackpots as they first thought.' A trial section was built in Cadogan Gardens to the rear in 1934, with red tile facings to concrete mullions, rather than the bronze effect of the main structure. The spandrel panels were covered with hinged bronze casements with the intention that they could be painted in different colours or even filled with wallpaper. The pleasing double-curved corner resulted from London County Council road planners. The intention was to fill the whole island site, but the north-west corner was never completed. The whole building was thoroughly overhauled by John McAslan in 2000.

Alan Powers

Lancaster Buildings

Location: High Street, Newcastle-under-Lyme, Staffordshire
Designed by: Hickton and Madeley of Hatherton Street, Walsall
Opened: 1940
Listed: Grade II

This block of 12 shops and offices was erected by Newcastle Corporation, which held a national competition to select a design worthy of this high-profile location. Costing £35,000, it had a steel frame and reinforced concrete awnings. An imposing composition, its simple elegance remains satisfying today.

The island building addresses four streets with shops onto each. The shop fronts are distinguished by Verte Tinos marble stall risers, large plate glass windows, travertine marble surrounds and a pierced concrete canopy, formerly with glass block, that steps with the streets. Above are red brick elevations, recessed rounded corners with curved horizontal windows; three sculpted roundels feature local industries, flanked by star motifs. The office entrance has a columnar doorcase in golden travertine, with bronze doors, and, unusually, rises through the canopy. Inside is a bronze balustraded staircase around a lift, travertine-lined walls and a central courtyard. Alterations have led to some loss of original fabric.

Katriona Byrne with research by Jo Prinsen

Oakwood Fish Bar

Location: 492 Roundhay Road, Leeds
Opened: 1940
Listed: Grade II

This Vitrolite shop front was installed onto a Victorian building for Garside and Pearson, listed as fried fish dealers in 1940. Dating to pre-1908, vitrolite had been used to clad UK shopfronts for 13 years, injecting high streets with instant glamour and modernity. This is a remarkable example, in its original design and its survival.

The tiny frontage is entirely of black Vitrolite. The stall riser is continuous with the main front which features a large circular window, its glass etched to resemble waves. The Vitrolite panels are fixed to the structural frame, with chrome framing to the openings. The fascia has distinctive Art Deco 'go-faster' stripes, which turn 90 degrees and continue down onto the front. The sign is composed of individual raised letters in metal and neon. The recessed entrance has Vitrolite cheeks and soffit, and double timber doors. Inside are yellow Vitrolite-clad walls.

Katriona Byrne

1950 – 1959

Chrisp Street market and shopping precinct

Location: Tower Hamlets, London
Designed by: Frederick Gibberd
Opened: 1951
Listed: Clock tower listed Grade II

This was the first modern pedestrianised shopping precinct to be built in England (Coventry's was planned earlier but built later). This part of the Stepney-Poplar reconstruction area identified in the County of London Plan (1943) hosted the Festival of Britain's Live Architecture Exhibition in 1951. The idea of showcasing a real piece of city under renewal was the brainchild of Frederick Gibberd, who was then asked to design the market and precinct for the area, later named the Lansbury estate.

Superseding a nearby street market, Gibberd's scheme included 38 shops with maisonettes and flats above, two pubs and clock tower arranged around an open marketplace. The understated brick elevations of the buildings with their Scandinavian detailing, the wide pedestrianised parades of shops set behind tiled arcades and the vertical punctuation of the jazzy clock tower, make its influence on the commercial centres of the new towns which followed shortly after unmistakable.

Posy Metz

Dingles Department Store

Location: 40-46 Royal Parade, Plymouth
Designed by: Thomas Tait of Sir John Burnet, Tait & Partners
Opened: 1951

Dingles was Thomas Tait's last completed work and the first department store to be built in Britain after the Second World War. It seized the best site in Patrick Abercrombie and James Paton Watson's grid plan on the corner of Royal Parade and Armada Way, the great public space running through the new city centre. The composition – strong horizontal bands of stonework and windows, asymmetrically balanced against the vertical tower – refines the modernism that Tait developed through the 1930s. Dingles is beautifully and minimally detailed in contrasting Portland and Ham stone and its finish and form influenced the style of the 1950s city centre.

The upper floors were added by Burnet Tait's Bristol partnership in the 1970s and further remodelled after a fire in 1988. Dingles was sold to House of Fraser in 1971 and leased to Sports Direct in 2018 by the property company British Land. Its future is uncertain.

Jeremy Gould

104

RIGHT Perspective view of Dingles by Sally McClellan

David Greig

Location: St George's Street, Canterbury, Kent
Designed by: Robert Paine and Partners
Opened: 1954
Listed: Grade II

The post-war reconstruction of the eastern part of the old city of Canterbury was neither a critical nor a popular success. Its set-piece shopping square has vanished and only a few fragments remain of its buildings. The best of these, however, has survived redevelopment and was recently restored. Built for David Greig, a chain of butchers, the shop and its adjacent travertine-clad service and flat block were designed by Robert Paine, the founder and head of the Canterbury School of Architecture and the architect of a number of small houses and bungalows in and near the city.

The shop was a single-glazed space, open to its concrete zig-zag roof. When illuminated at night, its canopy, lit from within, its sheets of clear and clouded glass along the side lane elevation and its stylish lettering and logo brought Festival of Britain cheer to visitors entering the city's shopping street from the east.

Timothy Brittain-Catlin

Lewis's

Location: Ranelagh Street, Liverpool
Designed by: Gerald de Courcy Fraser
Opened: 1956
Listed: Grade II

Superbly sited between Liverpool's two railway termini and facing the Adelphi Hotel, until 2010 this was the last surviving example of the national Lewis's chain that began in Liverpool. It now lies largely abandoned.

In a simplified classical style, the Portland stone elevations have fluted stone balconies and magnificent incised gilt Roman letters saying LEWIS'S. Above the main doors are carved stone panels by Sir Jacob Epstein, featuring members of his family, and looming over them a bronze nude, *Liverpool Resurgent*, also by Epstein; the sculpture is known locally as Dickie Lewis. The store, the last in the city with lift attendants, had tiled floors, low ceilings and was a navigational challenge. It was famous for household goods in the basement and its Christmas grottos, something Lewis's invented in 1879 – thence the idea spread to America, one of many cultural exchanges through this port city. The restaurant, tiled by Carter's of Poole, now serves a hotel on the upper floors.

Andrew Crompton

Maples

Location: 83-85 Queen's Road
and 30 Triangle West, Bristol
Designed by: James Wilson
Mackintosh
Opened: 1956

Furniture stores need large sites and easy access because their goods are bigger than those in most stores. They gather on the edge of shopping areas, in Bristol historically on the prosperous west side of town. Maples opened their first store in London in 1841. When in 1950 the company leased a store at 93–95 Whiteladies Road in Bristol, it claimed to be 'the largest furnishing house in the world', with 24 stores.

In April 1954 Maples applied to build larger showrooms on a bomb site at the western apex of The Triangle, where the steep slope admitted access from two levels. The company collapsed in 1997, and the building now houses cafés and a gym. James Wilson Mackintosh was a Bristol architect who had earlier worked for W. H. Watkins & Partners, specialising in shops and cinemas either side of the war. The store is striking for its minimal yet monumental classical façades.

Elain Harwood

Coventry Shopping Precinct

Location: Lower Precinct, Coventry
Designed by: Coventry City Architect's
Department: Donald Gibson, Arthur
Ling, Terence Gregory
Opened: In phases, 1956–61
Listed: Grade II

The radical post-war plans for Coventry's blitzed city centre introduced the concept of traffic-free shopping to the country as early as 1941. Gibson's cruciform pedestrian precinct offered open squares, rooftop parking and art, from carved murals to Trevor Tennant's *Lady Godiva* trotting out above Broadgate. The precinct's unifying heights, rhythms and materials were modelled in the Corporation's development of Broadgate House: buff brick, with travertine, Westmorland Green slate and warm Hornton stone detailing. From the brick of Broadgate, green slate and strip windows dominate the main descending axis, where set-back link blocks originally offered two-level shopping.

From 1955, Arthur Ling brought more varied materials, and a lighter, smaller scale, particularly to Market Way and the western Lower Precinct, with its elevated circular café and successful two-tier shopping. The precinct's north–south axis has suffered from various redevelopments, and the southern end of this axis and the intimate City Arcade is now under threat.

Sarah Walford

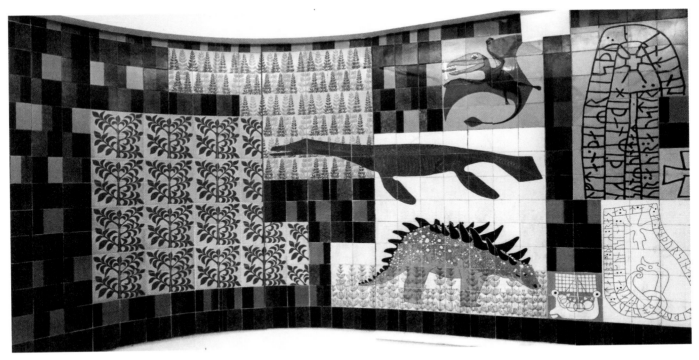

Central Parade

Location: Walthamstow, London
Designed: F. G. Southgate,
Borough Surveyor
Opened: 1958
Listed: Grade II

A joyous chunk of Festival style, Central Parade stands at the junction of Hoe Street and Church Hill. When this prominent corner site was hit by a V1 rocket in 1944, the council kept its redevelopment in-house and the result was a striking piece of commercial streetscape. The new building combined shops, housing, a bank with offices above and, unusually, a public hall.

There is a full house of contemporary motifs, from colourful geometric tiles by Carter and Co. to atomic bobbles on wiry balcony fronts. A sinuous, crinkle-cut canopy of reinforced concrete shelters the shopping parade along Hoe Street and the corner of the building is punctuated with a wall of heraldic tile-work and the ultimate centrepiece for post-war civic placemaking, a clocktower. A building which cannot fail to lift the spirits, it is a tonic to this corner of Walthamstow. Central Parade was listed in 2017.

Posy Metz

Coventry Retail Market

Location: Queen Victoria
Road, Coventry
Designed by: Coventry City
Architect's Department; designs
by Douglas Beaton, Ralph Iredale
and Ian Crawford
Opened: 1958
Listed: Grade II

Coventry's circular market is one of the earliest post-war markets that survives relatively intact. Basement storage, 200 stalls and rooftop parking offered up-to-date facilities for shoppers and stallholders. Designed for easy circulation, the stalls, some still with original signs, are arranged in concentric rings around the central area. Small shop units, some inward and some outward facing, form the building's perimeter, with a continuous clerestory above. V-shaped concrete columns support the concrete roof and car park. Although this no longer has its heated access ramp, it still links to other rooftop parking, part of Coventry's post-war traffic segregation. The central area offers seating and additional light from a raised clerestory. It now contains the merry-go-round, which was originally moved through the precinct as new sections opened, to lure shoppers through their children. Colourful nautical figures from the demolished fish market decorate the central supports and a Socialist Realist mural by Dresden art students remains above the market offices.

Sarah Walford

Woodside Shopping Centre

Location: Woodside Way, Glenrothes, Fife
Designed by: Wheeler & Sproson
Opened: 1958

The first new towns were built as a series of neighbourhoods, each based on a primary school with a parade of shops to supply housewives with their daily needs and a community centre or public house for sociability. The shops were set back from the road for pedestrian safety, with arcades to give some shelter from the weather. Woodside, designed in 1952 and opened by the Queen, survives better than most, thanks to the strength of its clean architectural lines, though one-stop convenience stores have displaced the original variety of separate shops. There are two parades, with the road on one side and a barrel-vaulted community hall on the other, and Wheeler & Sproson also designed nearby housing. Glenrothes was the first town to appoint an artist to work in the community, David Harding. His young assistants included Hugh Graham, who added the sculpture Ivy Pillar in the centre of the square in 1976.

Elain Harwood

Cwmbrân New Town Shopping Centre

Location: Torfaen
Designed by: J. C. P. West, Gordon Redfern, Cwmbrân Development Corporation
Opened: 1958 onwards

Cwmbrân was one of the first and most interesting new town centres in post-war Britain. As at Stevenage, Cwmbrân Development Corporation (CDC) took the new commercial centre as an opportunity to revolutionize the consumer experience and provide a regional destination.

Pedestrianisation, public transport and extensive car parking combined with a network of 'streets' and arcades to maintain the feel of a historic hub. Sleek lines of low-rise shops, orientated for optimum natural light, were punctuated by landmark buildings such as the Congress Theatre, David Evans and Monmouth House, with its towering William Mitchell sculpture. Communal squares at each end of the main thoroughfare, with bandstands, water gardens, public art and planting, provide areas for relaxation.

The centre was sold to a private company in 1985 when the CDC was dissolved. Much is earmarked for redevelopment including Gwent Square and the Water Gardens, the latter denied listing despite campaigning by the C20 Society and others.

Susan Fielding

Stevenage Town Centre

Designed by: Leonard Vincent,
Stevenage Development Corporation
Opened: 1959

Stevenage was Britain's first new town and the first to have a pedestrianised town centre. This was proposed in 1947 but only confirmed in 1954, after local residents overturned revised proposals that included a road, and Leonard Vincent (the new, young chief architect) had led a visit to the Lijnbaan precinct in Rotterdam, opened in 1953 with 70 shops.

Vincent's team produced every detail, including the layout, elevations, materials, landscaping and street furniture, leading to an unusually unified shopping complex. The development was planned to be intimate in scale, with around 100 shops situated on a single main route (Queensway), two smaller pedestrian ways and a Town Square with a (listed) clock tower, fountain and platform for public meetings. This core (extended northwards in the 1960s) is a conservation area and essentially survives, but there are worries for its future with the prospect of new housing to the south and west.

Emily Cole

Knight & Lee

Location: Palmerston Road, Southsea
Designed by: Cotton, Ballard and Blow
Opened: 1959
Listed: Grade II

This department store, part of the reconstruction of Portsmouth's war-damaged commercial centre, was built for John Lewis Partnership, who had acquired the local business in the 1930s and kept its name. The design, materials and detailing are high quality, the work of a successful post-war commercial and retail practice. A long front elevation of reflective glazing contrasts with the brick returns and towers but are tied together visually by the exposed concrete frame. Shopfronts are framed by stone and tile-clad surrounds and entrances decorated with bright mosaics, all set beneath a sweeping, continuous concrete canopy, offering shelter for shoppers. Inside, the original main stair, with its terrazzo floor and hardwood handrail, zig-zags up to the shop floors. The store closed in 2019 and was finally listed in 2021, after being turned down in 2006. The building is being converted for mixed use, including café, bar, cinema, offices, hotel and gym.

Coco Whitaker

Pannier Market

Location: Market Avenue, Cornwall Street, New George Street, Plymouth
Designed by: Herbert Walls & Paul Pearn; Albin Chronowicz, engineer
Opened: 1959
Listed: Grade II

Surely the best of Plymouth's post-war buildings and the only major building in the new city centre by locally-based architects, although Walls & Pearn were both Liverpool graduates and Chronowicz, an expert on shell structures, from Poland. Surrounded by outward-facing shops on three sides, a great column-free central space, some 40ft (12m) high and 224ft (68m) long with a 152ft (46m) span, is lit by seven rows of curved northlights formed in thin concrete shells perched on massive concrete portal frames. The exterior was clad in chequerboard-pattern concrete squares and sea-green enamelled panels all enlivened by striped shop awnings; the interior was painted white, sky blue and pale yellow and the two porches further embellished with murals by local artist David Weeks.

Subsequent restorations have diluted the original colours and cladding but the market still thrives, helped by an imaginative flexible letting policy and the mixed community of students and Plymothians that now surrounds it.

Jeremy Gould

DEPARTMENT STORES

Department stores evolved as a distinct architectural form in the second half of the nineteenth century, and by the First World War had grown in ambition, both architecturally and in business terms, such that they would dominate the retail scene of the middle decades of the twentieth century. In Britain, the building type emerged from a number of different sources, but a typical pattern in many localities was for a successful drapery store to expand its product lines and eventually require more space, adding neighbouring premises and more floors, often in a piecemeal fashion. New, purpose-built accommodation for this kind of expanded drapery business began to appear in the 1860s, like Jeffery & Co.'s Compton House in Liverpool's Church Street (Messrs. Haigh & Co, 1866–7), but the first purpose-built department store is often held to be the Bon Marché in Brixton, South London, by H. Parsons and & W. H. Rawlings, 1876–7.

By the beginning of the twentieth century, steel-frame construction had become typical for this new building type, in common with other large commercial projects, with one of the first being The Coliseum in Stockton-on-Tees (W. Basil Scott of Redpath, Brown & Co, 1899–1901). The culmination of the first phase of department store evolution came with the construction of Selfridges on Oxford Street (Francis Swales and R. Frank Atkinson, 1907–09). Special exemption from the London Building Acts was secured in order to create larger, uninterrupted internal volumes than

the regulations allowed. This was important to Gordon Selfridge for the importation of American sales approaches into the staid British market. The steel-framed structure could become an unencumbered and efficient machine for selling, albeit one with theatre and glamour embedded throughout, from elevations and window displays, to merchandising techniques and special events.

The interwar years saw consolidation of the department store sector, shifting it away from standalone, local family businesses into the groupings that remain common today. Selfridges' enormous early success resulted in acquisition of many stores nationally, trading under their own name within the Selfridges Provincial Stores structure, including the old Bon Marché in Brixton. Debenhams had 70 stores by 1930 and House of Fraser began expansion from its Glasgow base in 1936. This was not just consolidation but expansion, too; the overall number of department stores roughly doubled to 500 between 1914 and 1950.

Although the chain stores and multiples grew significantly after the First World War, department stores more than held their own by diversification of product lines, competing directly with the middle market and cheaper prices that the chains offered, and providing for the exponentially growing suburbs and the suburban lifestyle of consumer durables and new furnishings that went with it. New stores were built in areas where the suburban

RIGHT Selfridges, Oxford Street, London, Daniel Burnham, 1909

population was growing fastest, not least in a ring around London in places such as Kingston, Croydon and Southend.

Architecturally, Selfridges created something of a template for the interwar department store, inside and out, and its giant order elevations became a popular inspiration for examples around the country. Neo-Georgian designs by architects such as Gerald de Courcy Fraser, working for the Lewis's group in cities including Leicester, were seen from the late 1920s. For smaller stores in locations beyond the big cities, versions of stripped classicism were popular, used across a maximum of three floors, often in faience, such as at the Bobby & Co. store in Folkestone (Reeve and Reeve of Margate, 1929–31).

The self-conscious modernity of landmark stores such as D.H. Evans on Oxford Street (Louis D. Blanc, 1934–7) and Kendal Milne's in Manchester (J. S. Beaumont with Louis D. Blanc, 1938–9) moved the building type forwards. Slender, continuous mullions were used in both cases as a substitute for columns or pilasters, so that scale and grandeur were evoked without the use of overt classical language.

Examples of more rigorous modernity before the Second World War were rare, not least in terms of constructional techniques, but the new Peter Jones store by the John Lewis Partnership in Sloane Square, London (William Crabtree with Charles Reilly, 1932–9) was an exception

to these rules and was one of the clearest expressions of architectural modernism seen in Britain up until that time. Crabtree's design included one of the earliest uses of curtain walling in the country, with the glazed exterior standing proud of the concrete walls forming the superstructure. The tiered upper storeys of the building, set back from the main elevations, also became an influential architectural device for the building type.

Internally, there was a broad trend against the use of central light wells and stairwells, towards the 'horizontal' system deployed at Selfridges which pushed circulation to the edges, leaving as much uninterrupted floor space as possible, serviced by electric lighting and mechanical ventilation. This spatial arrangement was key to the new style of merchandising, with lots of stock on display, no longer behind counters, so customers were free to browse without the intrusion of sales assistants. Some exceptions to this included the John Lewis Partnership, which retained a preference for natural lighting, including at the new Peter Jones store. Artificial lighting was not an innovation in itself, but the new ways in which it was used to create specific kinds of sales environments made it more of an asset than a merely practical solution. The moderne interiors of Derry and Toms in Kensington High Street (C. A. Wheeler, 1929–33) saw the first use of concealed neon tube lighting, placed in the cornicing of the

LEFT Derry & Tom's, Kensington High Street, London, Bernard George, 1929-31

131

store's restaurant and fashion theatre to create a subtle, atmospheric effect.

Since the introduction of the first escalator (or 'revolving staircase') at Harrods in 1898, only the largest stores had used them, and typically only for communication between the lower floors and basement. The shift to mass adoption of escalators to all floors came with the D. H. Evans store of 1937, on Oxford Street, which used in its advertising the architectural spectacle of its central, criss-crossing escalator rigs serving all floors right at the centre of the store.

In the post-war period, competition from the multiples intensified and department stores were compelled to move even further into the mid-market. The number of independent stores declined at a faster rate as the groupings expanded their grip; consolidation and simplification of the sector and its architectural output were guiding principles. New stores were typically rebuilds (from war damage or otherwise) or relocations, especially from the 1970s onwards when the move into malls as anchor tenants became a notable trend. This process began with the John Lewis Partnership when a redeveloped Jessops of Nottingham moved into the new Victoria Centre in 1972, followed by Bainbridge's moving into Eldon Square, Newcastle upon Tyne, in 1976. Architectural efforts were typically made in less expressive or decorative ways than before the war, partly as a result of shifts in architectural

fashion and partly as a conscious effort to not alienate the 'average' shopper.

Although steel framing remained the favoured constructional technique, concrete frames were important in the 1950s due to the steel shortage, and in London required in any case due to the byelaws. Curtain walling, despite the example offered by the Peter Jones store from the 1930s, did not become normalised in department stores, not least because of persistent concerns about how completely glazed fronts affected the merchandising of goods internally with a lack of solid wall for display space. The question of how much natural light was desirable for an optimised selling environment also remained an ongoing issue. Rigorously modern examples that used a curtain wall, such as the Tyrrell and Green store in Southampton (Yorke, Rosenberg and Mardall, 1954–6) were outliers in a sector that relied instead on more pragmatic approaches.

There remained a stylistic preference for more traditional styles, albeit in a stripped-down manner. Examples of total historicism were comparatively rare, but the use of traditional materials such as Portland stone – used in the rebuilt Plymouth, for instance – and the absence of overt modernist detailing was typical of a slightly more conservative approach, even as elevations were simplified with cleaner lines and more horizontal emphasis. Stores such as Lewis's in Liverpool (Gerald de Courcy Fraser,

RIGHT John Lewis, Oxford Street, Slater and Uren, 1955-60, showing Barbara Hepworth's sculpture 'Winged Figure' added in 1963

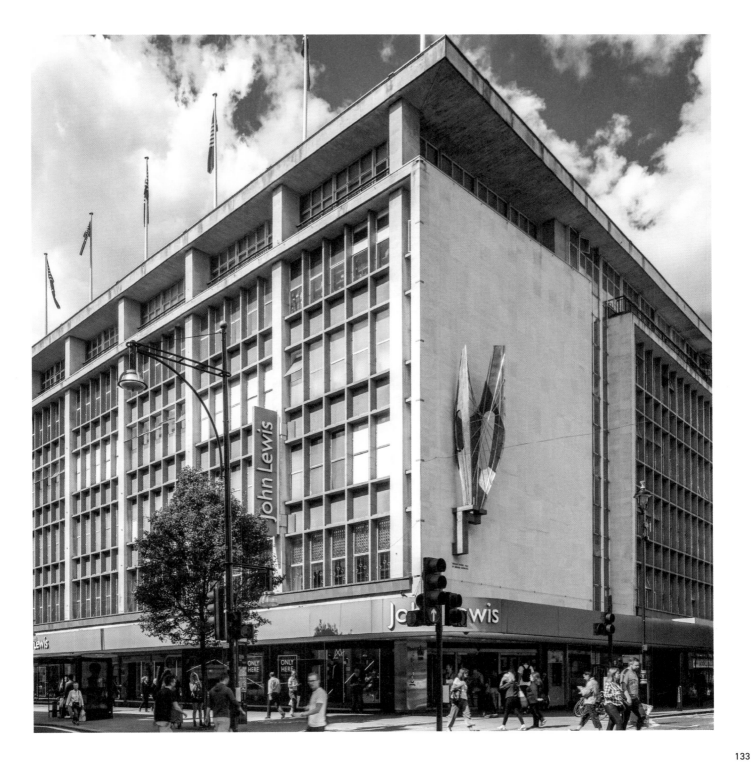

1948–58), with their post-war take on classicism, were not representative of wider trends. Far more common was the use of 'softer' forms of modernism, such as at Knight & Lee, Southsea (1956–9, Cotton, Ballard & Blow), which drew on Festival of Britain reference points of playful detailing, warm textures of brick, and gentle massing. John Lewis's new Oxford Street store (Slater and Uren, 1955–60) connected with a similar set of traditions, creating a more restrained, civic presence by using Portland stone.

Examples of 'high' modernism were far less common. Of the Yorke, Rosenberg and Mardall examples in Sheffield, Southend and Southampton, only the 1961–3 Cole Brothers (John Lewis Partnership) of Sheffield survives largely unaltered. A Denys Lasdun design for Peter Robinson on The Strand in London (1959), of blank white walls below curtain glazing, was demolished in 1996. There were many more examples of stores that achieved a distinct but modest modernist architectural effect from the expression of different functions and an overall simplicity in design, such as Owen Owen (now Primark) in Coventry (Rolf Hellberg and Maurice H. Harris, 1951–4) and Plummer Roddis/ Debenhams in Guildford (George Baines & Syborn, 1963–8).

Internally, the continuous or horizontal floorplan became dominant, with lifts and even escalators pushed to the edges of the plan although, as before the war, the John Lewis Partnership bucked this trend by retaining central light wells in most cases. Self-selection became the norm from the mid-1950s, as another means of simplifying the shopping experience and attracting more working-class customers. Sales floors were, on the whole, spaces of uninterrupted volumes, artificially lit and ventilated, and often with decorative schemes of the pre-war era hidden within encased columns and suspended ceilings. Exceptions to this functional trend emerged much later in the post-war era, with Harrods's refurbishment of 1987–97 (including the grandiose Egyptian Hall of 1991) seeking a revival of an earlier era of retailing theatre. A return to bold, modern architectural commissioning for store interiors, such as at Selfridges in Manchester (Stanton Williams, 2002) and Birmingham (Future Systems, 2003), has only occurred at the very top of the market, with neutrality and plainness remaining the norm elsewhere.

A trend for external sculpture took hold in the immediate post-war years, typically with the aim of saying something about the locality in which the store was embedded, or about the nature of the business, or both. Jacob Epstein's *Liverpool Resurgent*, positioned over the entrance to the newly rebuilt Lewis's in Liverpool and unveiled in 1956, took the form of a naked male figure standing in triumphant pose on the prow of a ship. John Lewis's new Oxford Street store unveiled Barbara Hepworth's *Winged Figure* (1963) for the Holles Street elevation, a few years after the store itself opened. The commission from John Spedan Lewis was for a work to represent 'the idea of common ownership and common interests', though Hepworth's own interpretation was that she had evoked a 'sensation of freedom'.

The size of department stores' operations created the need for a number of ancillary buildings to service them, not least off-site warehousing that could either be nearby or distant enough to service a regional distribution system. One of the most celebrated post-war examples, with its expressive shell concrete roof, was the John Lewis warehouse in Stevenage (Yorke, Rosenberg and Mardall, 1963). The provision of customer car parking, naturally a crucial part of the evolution of the business model during the second half of the twentieth century, began modestly in the 1930s with surface car parks at places such as Welwyn Department Stores, which offered free parking over an underground air raid shelter. The post-war period saw multi-storey car parks integrated with newly built stores, beginning with Selfridges in London, which built a car park extension of 1958–60 on Edwards Mews, known as the Lex Selfridge Garage (Sydney Clough, Son & Partners), and Cole Brothers in Sheffield (Yorke, Rosenberg and Mardall, 1963), a trend that was overtaken somewhat by the 1970s move into malls where extensive, integrated provision was shared by a large number of businesses. More typical for the established store locations was the creation of detached multi-storey car parks nearby, such as the Welbeck Street multi-storey (Michael R. Blampied & Partners, 1970–1), developed by Debenhams to service its Oxford Street flagship store.

In the twenty-first century, semi-integrated store/car park schemes, such as Selfridges in Birmingham's Bull Ring and John Lewis at Liverpool ONE (store by John McAslan + Partners, bridge and car park by WilkinsonEyre, engineered by Arup, 2005–08) continued this tradition as part of the 'outdoor mall' concept, with detached parking intended to service these stores, linking them with architecturally ambitious covered pedestrian bridges. As the planning system swung against out-of-town malls, favouring redeveloped central locations from the late 1990s onwards, the department store experienced a late and perhaps final flowering. The global pandemic accelerated the use of internet shopping, and it is likely that only a much smaller number of sites can survive long term; those that offer the architectural spectacle, tangible services and intangible sense of theatre that the online experience cannot.

Matthew Whitfield

135

1960 –
1969

House of Fraser (Rackhams), Birmingham

Location: Corporation Street, Birmingham
Designed by: Philip Bennett, T. P. Bennett & Son; engineers, Ove Arup & Partners
Opened: 1960

This store, designed for Harrods who bought Rackhams in 1955, and who were in turn taken over by House of Fraser in 1959, opened in phases between 1959 and 1960 and was extended in 1966. It was at the centre of shopping life in Birmingham for decades.

Built of reinforced concrete, eight storeys high, it occupies most of a city block, including an arcade of shops, offices and a vehicle ramp to loading bays inside. The shop windows have granite surrounds with concrete canopies. The elevations are in Portland stone, each having a distinctive treatment: Temple Row and Corporation Street feature concertina glazing, with once-coloured spandrel panels, giving the building a delightful exuberance; small square windows proliferate.

In the 1980s the blue glazing was renewed in blue and black. The interior retains some original finishes and murals. The curvilinear main staircase, clad in blue Belgian marble, acted as a catwalk for fashion shows. A Certificate of Immunity from listing was granted in 2021.

Katriona Byrne with research by Jo Prinsen

I. Camisa & Son

Location: 61 Old Compton
Street, Soho, London
Opened: 1961

Fratelli Camisa was originally opened by brothers Ennio and Isidoro Camisa at 66 Old Compton Street in 1929, when Soho was a meeting place for Italian immigrants escaping fascism. The shop closed after they were both interned during the war, re-opening in Berwick Street around 1948. Later, the brothers parted ways and Isidoro opened I. Camisa & Son on its current site in 1961. An authentic *generi alimentari* selling Italian produce, which was then not widely available in supermarkets, it became an institution.

The full-height display window, with travertine marble surround, was packed with products and originally salami, strings of onions and panettone also hung outside. Neon replaced the 1960s block lettering but the shopfront with its green canopy, delivery bicycle and Italian flag sign remain. A public campaign in 2022 has helped this rare survivor of the continental delis and coffee bars that served Soho's European communities to survive – for now.

Susannah Charlton

Birds Bakery

Location: 4 Poultry, Nottingham
Designed by: United Shopfitters
of Bristol
Opened: 1961
Listed: Grade II

As a child, my Friday tea-time treat was a cream cake from Birds. The East Midlands confectionery chain, founded by Derby ex-servicemen in 1919, reached Nottingham in 1961 and my native Beeston in 1966. The central Nottingham shop was just off the Market Square, where all the stores are set behind an arcade, first noted by the diarist Celia Fiennes in 1697 but subsequently rebuilt. Birds is the only one where the supporting columns are clad in blue and white mosaic, with red and grey mosaic to the party wall. A curved glass shop front stretches from floor to ceiling, its double doors and display sections framed in chrome. Birds' delicate glass display shelving, pendant lights and signage were features across the chain until a heavy-handed refurbishment programme in 2017. The central Nottingham branch was listed and spared but closed in 2020 when most of the interior fittings were removed.

Elain Harwood

Central Market
Swansea

Location: Oxford Street, Swansea
Designed by: Sir Percy Thomas & Son
Opened: 1961

Swansea was devastated by heavy bombing during the Second World War and the market was one of many shops, offices and other buildings destroyed in the town's hitherto successful commercial centre. The market's replacement, not built until 15 years after the end of the war, is in the style prevalent after the Festival of Britain.

The indoor market is the largest one in Wales and is nestled within a U-shaped block of shops and offices. The hangar-like roof of the market, engineered by W. S. Atkins, has a clear span of 190ft (60m) and the efficient steel arch beams that support it are subtly tapered in response to the bending and thrust profile. The gable ends are glazed along with the lower sections of the vault and fill the spectacular space with natural light. This is the place to buy your laverbread, and to feel the spirit of Swansea.

Jonathan Vining

The Viking Centre

Location: 38 Bede Precinct, Jarrow
Designed by: Shingler Risdon
Associates
Opened: 1961

Sam Chippindale and Arnold Hagenbach, founders of Arndale, built only small shopping parades until in 1958 they secured a deal with Jarrow council for a full-scale pedestrian precinct. It was a T-shaped development of 93 shops that led most multiples to abandon the nearby high street. The deal was a coup for Arndale, from which the council gained only £8,000 a year, rising to £14,000 over 178 years. But as the financial expert Oliver Marriott admitted, 'The shops themselves, built in stages, readily found tenants and the liveliness of this modern mart in the heart of Jarrow boosted the low morale of the town', following the chronic unemployment of the 1930s. 'The centre claimed the busiest pie shop in the North-East.' The open parades were designed in a late-Festival style, mostly of brick, with canopies giving some shelter from the rain and more elaborate curtain walling to three-storey units at the entrances.

Elain Harwood

John Wherritt

Location: 5–7 Eastborough, Scarborough
Opened: c.1962

John Wherritt is a family business selling gifts and jewellery, founded in the nineteenth century, which expanded in the early 1960s by knocking two shops into one. The plan could date from the 1930s: an island display case flanked by angled entrances to a door concealed behind, and large canted windows on tiled stall risers with a run of narrow toplights that extend across the door.

A greater distinction comes from the choice of materials and signage. The floor is of terrazzo, with bold chunks of black and brown marble, the latter the colour of the stall riser tiles – the only match in the composition. The contrasting timber fascia is painted a different brown. What really appeals, however, is the original 1960s signage, especially that encouraging us to 'walk round'; with so much stock in this Aladdin's cave, it is physically impossible to do so, making that large display space essential.

Elain Harwood

Cole Brothers

Location: Barkers Pool,
Cambridge Street, Sheffield
Designed by: Yorke, Rosenberg
and Mardall
Opened: 1963
Listed: Grade II

In 1963, after 124 years trading at what is still known as Cole's Corner, Sheffield's premier department store moved its entire stock 300 yards in just two days. The new store for Cole Brothers (by then part of the John Lewis Partnership) was opened on 17 September by the Lord Mayor, who used tailors' shears to cut a white ribbon that matched the white modernity of the architects' trademark Belgian-tiled façades. The building dimensions follow the module of these white tiles, so that none had to be cut and the whole thing appears pleasingly crisp as a result. Projecting panels are covered in dark brown Italian glass mosaic, and grey Spanish granite clads the ground floor. The attached continuous ramped car park for 400 vehicles has direct access to the store at every floor and a more brutalist, windowless rear elevation 131 tiles wide.

Andrew Jackson

Castle House Co-op

Location: Angel Street, Sheffield
Designed by: George S. Hay,
Co-op Architect's Department
Opened: 1964
Listed: Grade II

Castle House was built for the Brightside & Carbrook Co-Operative Society and named after Sheffield Castle, the remains of which had been discovered nearby during construction of the Society's previous store in 1927. That store was gutted in the Blitz of 1940. Subsequent delays aided the development of a sophisticated replacement, that referenced models in Chicago and Amsterdam, with blind upper façades, faced in granite, that allowed for goods inside to be artificially lit without distraction (see page 244). The ground floor housed a food hall, and above followed three floors of departments, including a record bar with listening booths. The helical central stair led to a stylish restaurant with seating for 300 and signposted by a wall-mounted sculpture *Fish and Fowl* (stainless steel for the fish and copper sheet for the fowl) by the Co-op's in-house interior designer Stanley Layland. The building now houses a popular bar, food court and creative office space.

Andrew Jackson

Evan Roberts

Location: Queen Street, Cardiff
Designed by: T. Alwyn Lloyd and
Gordon, Alex Gordon & Partners
Opened: In two phases, 1958–64

Alex Gordon's practice produced several curtain-walled buildings of quality in Cardiff in the 1960s, including award-winning university laboratories, the well-regarded former Wales Gas Board offices, and a new store for the family outfitters Evan Roberts. The last was a fine example of the international modern style, conceived rationally in terms of the technology of the time. It had a beautifully detailed, continuous expanse of curtain walling to the upper levels that curved around the corner of Queen Street, opposite Cardiff Castle. The interplay between the white mullions and the well-proportioned black panels alluded to historical precedents of 'black and white' buildings next to castles of old. Inset balconies, informally placed at each upper level, allowed customers to take samples outside to better judge their colours, while promoting interaction with the street – a civic gesture. Demolished in 1985 for redevelopment, Cardiff could ill afford to lose buildings of such quality, and at such a young age.

Jonathan Vining

Habitat, Chelsea

Location: Fulham Road, London
Interior designed by: Terence Conran
and Oliver Gregory
Opened: 1964

Habitat revolutionised the way a generation lived. Terence Conran started his career working on the Festival of Britain and believed passionately that good, accessible design improves everyday life. As well as modern design classics and Conran's own 'Summa' furniture range, Habitat marketed simple, useful homewares reflecting Scandinavian style and rural French life to the newly affluent of the Swinging Sixties. The quarry-tiled floor, whitewashed brick walls, white-painted tongue-and-groove ceiling and spotlights of the Fulham Road interior were the template when Habitat became a chain, selling a simplified range. From 1966 they produced a catalogue, *Habitat by Post*, which presented a new, relaxed way of life, not just products. No fashionable home was without its flokati rug, bean bag, chicken brick or pasta jar. Conran was adept at transforming abandoned buildings, rather than building afresh. In 1973 the original store became the more upmarket Conran Shop, before moving to the refurbished Michelin House opposite.

Susannah Charlton

Jarnac Court

Location: Dalkeith, Midlothian
Designed by: Robert James Naismith,
office of Sir Frank Mears and Partners
Opened: 1964

Robert James Naismith flipped comfortably from vernacular-inspired 'conservative surgery', in the Patrick Geddes tradition, to something closer to the 'vernacular Modernism' of Robert Matthew. The centrepiece of his work as Burgh Architect of Dalkeith is a pedestrianised central redevelopment, the striking group of three buildings around Jarnac Court (1960–64) forming the most substantial part. Naismith's own 'vernacular Modernism' is certainly present here, with the convex arc of flats over shops divided by rubbly spine walls and set off by a sweeping, timber-lined canopy. The corner office block is strongly framed in concrete – almost Brutalist but rendered a touch more 'contextual' by the stone panel infill.

Despite the replacement of original hard landscaping and the refacing of the remaining office building, Jarnac Court has worn remarkably well for a development of its kind and era. It would be reassuring, however, if Midlothian Council would reconsider its earlier decision to exclude it from the town's Conservation Area.

Euan McCulloch

MULTIPLES AND CHAIN STORES

As the British economy regained strength in the early 1920s, following the ravages and setbacks of the Great War, powerful multiple retailers (more widely understood by the North American term 'chains') began to transform high streets by building modern stores on prime sites, often superseding ancient inns and public houses. Their 'white ghostly façades' – a term coined by the architect Charles H. Reilly – contrasted strikingly with their older neighbours and were embellished with branding.

Before 1914 multiples generally commissioned local architects to design conventional buildings for the accommodation of branch stores. Boots the Chemist was unusual in developing alternative house styles: one in toffee-coloured terracotta rich with Renaissance-inspired motifs; the other in a half-timbered Tudorbethan style, adorned with arms and statuary. In each case, features of local relevance emphasised Boots' engagement with the host town or city. From 1914 W. H. Smith – another chain with middle-class credentials – cultivated a similar approach.

It was around 1922–4 that three retail giants – Burton, Marks & Spencer and F. W. Woolworth – began to exert their commercial dominance by buying freeholds in central locations and building in earnest. Their flat-roofed stores were of steel-framed construction with, by the 1930s, concrete floors. Façades were clad in 'ghostly' materials such as Empire Stone (reconstituted Portland) or glazed terracotta, otherwise known as faience. Since these businesses had abandoned traditional apprenticeships and the so-called living-in system, their store elevations were liberated from the constraints of domesticity. Lettering was affixed to parapets while decoration was concentrated around upper-floor windows. These lit stockrooms or, in the case of Burton, billiard halls. Marks & Spencer clung to classical styles through the 1930s, but for both Burton and Woolworth the stripped classicism of the early 1920s succumbed to a jazzy, Art Deco approach. Motifs could be playful: around 1932, for example, Burton erected a batch of stores with elephant-head capitals.

Marks & Spencer and Woolworth frequently enlarged their stores. In 1934, to simplify the process of lateral extension, Marks & Spencer commissioned Robert Lutyens to design a system of cladding comprising tiles measuring 10in (25cm) square. This was applied to around 40 stores, easily identified by their flat – almost Cubist – fronts. Those in Briggate, Leeds, and Oxford Street, London (the Pantheon site), were faced in sleek ebony granite rather than the usual pale artificial stone. In this respect they resembled a number of glamorous Burton stores, such as Hull and Catford, which had fronts of sparkling emerald pearl granite. Otherwise, these stores adhered to one of Burton's standard corporate styles. Designs were prepared by in-house architect Harry Wilson, followed by Nathaniel

RIGHT Boots' chief architect, Colin St Clair Oakes, designed this modern store for 72-78 High Street, Lewisham, in 1960. It opened in 1962 with self-service fixtures and a popular record department

157

Martin, who controlled one of the largest commercial architect's departments in the country by the late 1930s. Woolworth also had its own architect's department, led by William Priddle, followed by B. C. Donaldson, while Marks & Spencer's architect, E. E. Shrewsbury, tended to farm out the design process to favoured architectural firms dotted around the country, including W. A. Lewis & Partners (later Lewis & Hickey) and James M. Munro & Son (later Munro & Partners).

British Home Stores, Littlewoods, the Fifty Shilling Tailors, the Times Furnishing Co. and C&A were among other prominent chains to build in a cinematic chain-store manner through the 1930s, favouring fenestration with a soaring, vertical emphasis and adding neon-tube lettering that evoked downtown Manhattan. Increasingly, however, chains found that they had to modify their transatlantic approach to satisfy local authorities and civic societies. For the big three – Burton, Woolworth and Marks & Spencer – this meant developing alternative house styles in the ever-respectable neo-Georgian idiom, although the local authorities in Wigan and Chester went a step further by pressing for neo-Elizabethan designs. Sainsbury's was one of the few multiples to build habitually in a neo-Georgian manner, with red brick fronts and sash windows. The reason was the continuing use of upper floors for staff accommodation. Sainsbury's interwar house style was,

therefore, ideally suited to its preferred position in the centre of suburban parades.

The display window was the single most important aspect of early chain stores, since customers tended to pick what they wanted – and could afford – by scrutinising ticketed items in windows before entering the premises. Lower-class shops consequently crammed windows with goods from top to bottom and plastered special offers to the glass. Bucking this trend in the early twentieth century, some tasteful shop fronts, with Art Nouveau or Arts and Crafts touches, were designed for chains like Jaeger, Kodak, W. H. Smith, G. A. Dunn and Austin Reed, all of whom – like Sainsbury's – aspired to attract better-off customers.

Between 1922 and 1926 Austin Reed's architect, Percy Westwood, was partnered by Joseph Emberton. Their Art Deco interiors for the flagship store in Regent Street are well known, but it was probably Emberton's work on the neon-lit façades of Austin Reed branches in Sheffield and Oxford Street that whetted his passion for architectural illumination. One of his most integrated works in this vein, Timothy Whites in Southsea, was erected in 1933 and replaced by the firm around 1937. By then Timothy Whites was building stores in a streamline moderne fashion, of red brick with white stone banding. More eye-catching moderne chain stores were created for Woolworth in Weymouth, Boots in Bexhill-on-Sea and BHS in Hammersmith.

LEFT Woolworth's store on Blackpool Promenade, next to the Tower, opened in 1938. It was designed by the company architect B. C. Donaldson and faced in cream coloured faience

Shortly after leaving Westwood, Emberton produced acclaimed shopfronts for Lotus & Delta shoe shops, indulging an interest in French engraved glass and jagged geometric forms sparked by his visit to the Exposition Internationale des Arts Décoratifs in Paris in 1925. This prompted other high-street shoe shops to abandon the restrained classicism that had dominated their shopfitting since 1918. At the popular end of the spectrum this culminated in two extensive arcade fronts, each with several island display windows, created in Oxford Street for Lilley & Skinner and Dolcis. These shops clamoured for attention with the notoriously garish fronts of wholesale bespoke tailors, such as Alexandre or Weaver to Wearer, which were emblazoned with fixed-price offers for made-to-measure suits.

More upmarket shoe shops were designed by Clive Entwistle for Russell & Bromley. These involved a subtle consideration of the night-time appearance of shops, with back-lit lettering, reflective soffits and, occasionally, curved non-reflective display windows of the type developed by E. Pollard & Co. and installed by Emberton at Simpson's in Piccadilly (now Waterstones). Entwistle may have been inspired by the elegant shopfronts designed by Wells Coates for Crysède and Cresta, and by J. Duncan Miller's work for Jaeger. Such shops abandoned massed display and treated windows as exhibition showcases, with lighting trained on choice merchandise, which was presented like works of art. The small Old Bond Street shopfront designed by Serge Chermayeff for Ciro Pearls in 1938 was another fine example, with mirrored ends and spindly supports creating the illusion of spaciousness.

The superiority of multiple shoe-shop design continued through the 1950s, only endling as Charles Clore's British Shoe Corporation exerted its stranglehold over the sector. The light-hearted colourful designs produced by Ellis Somake for Dolcis reflected the aesthetic popularised by the Festival of Britain, as did Patrick Gwynne's shopfront for Freeman Hardy & Willis in Catford, with its quirky displays and fingerpost signage. Bronek Katz produced more robustly modern designs for Bata and Richard Shops, whose Regent Street branch of 1949 set the tone for shopfitting in the womenswear sector for a full decade.

The most familiar architectural house styles of the 1930s, despite occasional echoes of Art Deco, were not reprised after 1945. Tight control by local authorities, working with their own architects alongside developers, meant that retailers could not build whatever they liked in prioritised towns: theoretically, at least, they had to comply with an urban aesthetic determined by planners. These conditions created tensions, but also resulted in fine chain stores in blitzed cities such as Plymouth and Coventry. After national building restrictions were lifted, some multiples attempted to implement new architectural house

RIGHT The rear salon of Dolcis, 22 Old Bond Street, was designed in 1952 by the company architect Ellis Somake with a mirror wall and sophisticated lighting

160

styles, principally by redeveloping their own freeholds in less controlled city centres. Burton and H. Samuel, for example, both erected stores with a high percentage of wall to window, with ribbon windows lighting stockrooms. H. Samuel's bunker-like store in Church Street, Liverpool, although a powerful presence, was at odds with the small and delicate nature of the firm's merchandise.

Following American precedent – with its reliance on efficient artificial lighting and air conditioning – chain stores, more than any other retailers, embraced the windowless façade in the 1960s. At the start of the decade, Michael Egan devised a system of metal cladding to modernise Victorian buildings for Saxone. By 1970 BHS, Littlewoods, Boots, C&A and others had created stores with blind frontages. The robust premises designed for C&A by Leach, Rhodes & Walker between 1969 and 1975, with hefty concrete frames covered in mosaic tiles, must be classed as one of the last truly distinctive architectural house styles to arrive on the high street. The Norwich store of 1970 exudes a remarkable air of contemporaneity in the hands of current occupant, Next. Although C&A and Marks & Spencer continued to build bulky town-centre stores into the late twentieth century, both companies abandoned their earlier efforts to maintain a distinctive architectural look.

Self-service existed before 1939, notably in cafeterias and in womenswear chains, but it was its enthusiastic adoption by the food sector in the 1950s and 1960s that radically changed the appearance of multiple shops. In particular, it led to the widespread introduction of the clearview window. Essentially, displays with closed backs were abandoned in favour of large windows and banks of armour-plated glass doors – later replaced by air curtains – offering an inviting view into shops. Initially, this helped to demystify self-service in grocery and provisions shops such as Sainsbury's, before becoming ubiquitous. Clearview windows (otherwise known as visual fronts) revealed that counters had been swept away and replaced by gondolas, Frigidaire units and checkouts.

As the new approach took hold, much pre-war shopfitting – including the beautifully tiled interiors of chains like Maypole Dairy, Lipton's and Home & Colonial Stores – was destroyed. Shopfronts belonging to Scotland's Buttercup Dairy Co., a house style created around 1915 with tiling by James Duncan, have survived only because the chain folded on the eve of self-service conversion. It is somewhat ironic that the most admired new food shop of the era, David Greig's provisions store in Canterbury, with its floating zig-zag roofline, still relied on old-fashioned counter service. Its elegance contrasted with the utilitarian approach of most purpose-built urban supermarkets, which seldom respected established building lines or heights. Supermarkets erected by Tesco and Asda in the 1960s matched, in both style and materials, the bargain-basement discounting policy of these businesses. Standards of building in the food sector were eventually elevated around 1970 by Sainsbury's, which began to build red brick stores with projecting boxy windows and, sometimes, murals alluding to the history of the region. These were created by Henry and Joyce Collins, Colchester-based sculptors who also produced colourful artwork for BHS.

After 1970 the retail landscape began to fragment, with the proliferation of covered shopping centres, out-of-town malls, superstores and retail parks. The processes whereby major multiples acquired new premises also changed. In towns they were now more likely to lease a unit provided by a developer and rely on external consultants to rework their shopfitting and branding. The launch and expansion of newcomers like Argos, Next and B&Q was often financed by exploiting the property value of older chains. As in-house architect's departments became increasingly redundant, the focus was on signage and logos rather than architecture. Nevertheless, the buildings of one or two late twentieth-century chains stand out, notably Sainsbury's.

Surprisingly, Asda was one of the first to abandon the functional simplicity of the 'big box' retail shed by building a barn-like store at South Woodham Ferrers in 1978, a homage to Essex vernacular and the strictures of the county's design guide. The 'barn' idea was embraced by Tesco, which began to add roofs and clock turrets to its stores. An alternative high-tech treatment was adopted by Sainsbury's in Canterbury and Camden in the course of the 1980s. Sainsbury's, who had an architectural committee for a time, which included architectural historians, aspired to elevate its architectural image and, to this end, held open competitions for its major superstores. The resulting designs tended to focus on entrance canopies, which provided an opportunity to reference the locality, for example with jaunty sails at Plymouth (1994) and a self-important portico in Harrogate (1993). This attempt at place-making was the modern equivalent of the Collins' murals or, going back further, Boots' statuary and coats of arms.

The climax of Sainsbury's architectural programme was an expensive and highly innovative superstore built on the Greenwich peninsula in 1999. With natural light pouring through its aerodynamic aluminium roof, the store incorporated a range of energy-saving devices such as solar panels, wind turbines and a reed bed that filtered rainwater for use in the lavatories. It was hailed as the future of superstore design and shortlisted for RIBA's Stirling Prize. However, just 15 years later, to howls of dismay, the building was flattened to make way for IKEA. Instead of inaugurating the sustainable superstore of the future, the episode was a sharp reminder of the fundamentally ephemeral nature of the retail landscape.

Kathryn A. Morrison

Former British Home Stores (BHS)

Location: 64 Princes Street, Edinburgh
Designed by: Robert Matthew,
Johnson-Marshall and Partners
Opened: 1965
Listed: Category B

Abercrombie and Plumstead's 1949 plan for Edinburgh proposed the reconstruction of the north side of Princes Street, the premier shopping street. This was refined by planners to include a continuous first-floor walkway – abandoned in 1979 after several buildings had made provision for it. Among them – described by the *Buildings of Scotland* as the 'first and best' – is the former British Home Stores, BHS's first flagship store in Scotland and a bespoke design. The main elevation is well detailed. The walkway level is denoted by a continuous band of polished black granite, originally featuring the store's name in an elegant typeface. Above is a secondary shop front. At the upper levels, bookended by blind York stone walls, a projecting volume has vertical strips of grey polished granite cladding. The architects insisted on an innovative interior with a central escalator well providing views through the store. The building has recently been refurbished for retail and hotel use.

Alistair Fair

Brighton Square

Location: The Lanes, Brighton
Designed by: Fitzroy Robinson
& Partners
Opened: 1966

Sensitively tucked into the famous Lanes is Brighton Square, a collection of shops, flats, paved square and discreet underground car park. The development repeats the footprint of the previous derelict buildings, and in its use of flint, hung tile and timber boarding reflects the local vernacular. Despite its politeness it is architecturally of its time and was the recipient of a Civic Trust Award. The open square later received a fountain by James Osborne, two leaping dolphins each with a child on board.

Until recently the square was a welcome breathing space after the claustrophobia of the tight twittens feeding into it. A new restaurant has enclosed the open space and erected dining pods, obscuring the fountain and banishing all non-customers to the outer perimeter. A planning application to strip the buildings of their tiles and timber boards, replacing them with render and grey cladding, was approved but not enacted.

Mark Hazell

Cumbernauld Town Centre

Designed by: Geoffrey Copcutt,
Cumbernauld Town Centre
Architect's Group
Opened: 1967

Cumbernauld was the first influential megastructure – a giant, multi-function building combining numerous urban functions – and, in Reyner Banham's view, the most complete expression of this idea in the world. Phase One combined a shopping centre, public-building functions, car park and transport interchange in a single, tiered, reinforced-concrete agglomeration of great external and internal complexity, dramatically crowned by a structurally separate range of penthouse flats supported on giant struts. More prosaically, this first covered multi-level centre provided a prototype for countless large indoor shopping precincts erected by speculative developers throughout the UK over the following decades.

Completed by Geoffrey Copcutt and his team as a steel-grey, bristling, space-age structure, it initially attracted vast numbers of 'eager visitors from Tucson to Vladivostok', but these gradually vanished as it was subjected to unsympathetic painting, plastic overcladding and crude truncations, which obscured its Brutalist boldness for most of its life. Total demolition is now threatened.

Miles Glendinning

The Fairwater Centre

Location: Cwmbrân New Town
Designed by: Gordon Redfern,
Cwmbrân Development Corporation
Opened: 1967

The largest of the neighbourhood unit centres in Cwmbrân, the Fairwater Centre was the first to be designed by Gordon Redfern as the new town's chief architect. Concerned by the particularly adverse weather of the region, 'high rainfall, mists, and variable winds', his aim was to physically and mentally cocoon shoppers during their visits. The result is fortress-like; a ring of two- and three-storey structures given an added defensive dimension through their hexagonal plan and the sharply angular parapets that extend above the rooflines. Within, the shop fronts nestle snugly below deep canopies.

As elsewhere, these small local shops have suffered economically in recent years, while the adventure playground in the centre, designed to entertain those forced to accompany their parents, has been removed. However, in the current search for more sustainable and community-based retail, Fairwater provides an excellent blueprint for what may be achieved and deserves a second lease of life.

Susan Fielding

1970 –
1979

Former Blackwell's Music Shop

Location: 38 Holywell Street, Oxford
Designed by: Gillespie, Kidd & Coia
Opened: 1970
Listed: Grade II

The former Blackwell's Music Shop is a rare example of the Glasgow-based firm of Gillespie, Kidd & Coia working on a post-war retail space, albeit one designed as part of the broader redevelopment of a gap site to provide new student and fellows accommodation for Wadham College, Oxford. The Royal Fine Art Commission and local planners' insistence that the new building's form replicate the garage it replaced stymied the architects' more assertive designs for a four storey, fully glazed façade.

The highlight of GK&C's shop is the generous octagonal light well at the heart of the building, which rises through two storeys, extruding from the roof deck above. The glazed funnel brilliantly offsets the shop's enclosed site, deep plan, and semi-subterranean nature, flooding the space with light.

After brief stints as a wine bar, then a restaurant, the former Music Shop is now home to Wadham's McCall MacBain Graduate Centre.

Tom Goodwin

Blackburn
Shopping Centre

Location: Church Street, Blackburn
Designed by: Building Design
Partnership (BDP)
Opened: 1970

Blackburn Shopping Centre was a town centre built for the new automotive age, using its sloping site to achieve total segregation of pedestrians and traffic. As a 1961 brochure boasted: 'It is a plan that has vision and courage. This is not a case of knocking down a street and rebuilding. Blackburn is going to have the sense and courage to knock down its whole town centre, re-plan it, and build in accordance with modern needs.' Within a faience-tiled structure, white tiles (detailed by Mary Smallbone of BDP) pick out the non-structural elements and bronze cladding the structural, giving an almost constructivist, multi-dimensional quality, breaking up its massive scale with a picturesque massing. The detailing was tough and urbane, and the centre was praised by Ian Nairn for having 'an industrial north style' – although he lamented that it necessitated demolition of so much of the Victorian cityscape.

Otto Saumarez Smith

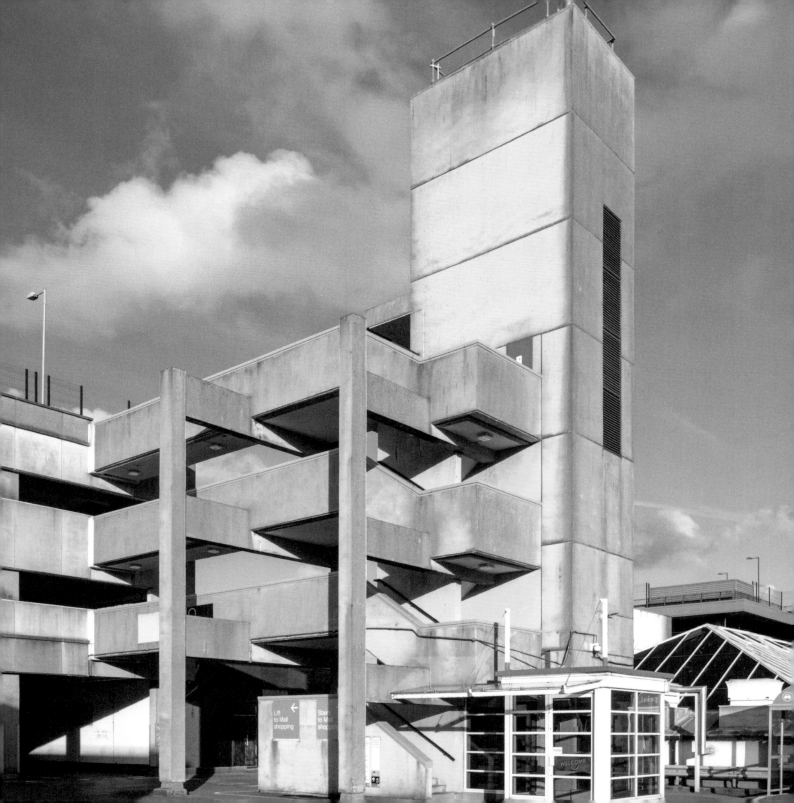

Escalade

Location: 191 Brompton Road, London
Opened: 1970

New department stores in London streets were rare in 1970. Escalade was the exception. With Harrods a looming presence nearby, it used American 'know-how' to update Swinging London.

Escalade developed the boutique towards the store within a store, described by critic Reyner Banham as 'a demonstrative chaos that makes an arcade a proper shambles'. This was done using space, Escalade featuring the tiers of semi-external escalators that were later to define Paris's Pompidou Centre, with shiny finishes of metals, glass and plastics. This was laid on a block of 1964 by Clifford Derwent & Partners that included flats on the upper floors. Escalade was created by Paul Young, originally from J. C. Penney's store in Greenfield, Massachusetts, selling everything from 'boutique clothing to butterscotch sundaes to foam rubber', with a hamburger restaurant, Japanese tea garden and hair salon. Emporio Armani took over in 2007, bringing in architects Four IV, but this has now closed.

Elain Harwood and Peter Ruback

Norco House

Location: George Street, Aberdeen
Designed by: Covell Matthews
Opened: 1970

Norco House, one of the most original and remarkable department store buildings of the 1960s, was designed for the Northern Co-operative Society. Above a continuous glazed shop front, storey-high bands of vertically ribbed concrete wrap around the building. They look a little like a concrete concertina, stretched taut. Massive, brooding, perhaps even introverted: these are the qualities of Aberdeen's historic granite architecture, translated into concrete.

This flagship store gave the Co-operative a modern image, just as Aberdeen's economy began to expand as a result of the 1970s oil boom. However, the Society overstretched itself: it left at the end of the 1980s. Subsequently, the building became home to John Lewis, but is now empty and its future uncertain. It would be a tragedy if a building described in *The Buildings of Scotland* as 'by a long way the most distinctive and impressive contribution of the 1960s to the city centre' were lost.

Alistair Fair

Former BOAC offices, Glasgow

Location: 83–85 Buchanan Street and 6 Mitchell Lane, Glasgow
Designed by: Gillespie, Kidd & Coia
Opened: 1970
Listed: Category B

A subtle response to its setting on a deep site, the building comprises a ground-floor showroom (originally for selling airline tickets) and offices above. The elevations are organised in three clearly articulated parts. At the base, the glazed shop front matches the height of its older neighbours; inside, there were originally complex sloping ceilings with dramatic inbuilt lighting. The shop front is topped by a deep incised band, above which three floors of offices project confidently forward, with octagonal windows set into the copper-clad elevation. The top of the building steps back again before being crowned by a projecting horizontal band.

The result has a pleasing sculptural complexity: a sense of depth and mass which echoes Glasgow's Victorian buildings. And, in following the scale of its neighbours without recourse to pastiche, it demonstrates a contextual turn in Gillespie Kidd & Coia's work, which also found expression in their contemporaneous buildings at Wadham College, Oxford.

Alistair Fair

Heffers

Location: Trinity Street, Cambridge
Designed by: Austin-Smith: Lord
Opened: 1970

Completed in 1970, Heffers bookshop in Trinity Street, Cambridge, replaced its former five-storey shop in Petty Cury after the Trinity College bursar, John Bradfield, had acquired a complete island block opposite their main gate in 1964. Historic façades were retained, and a podium created at first-floor level behind, from which rises the Architects Co-Partnership's Wolfson Court. Heffers slotted in beneath the podium, with an ingenious design by Austin-Smith: Lord on three levels, leading browsers into an atrium gallery with show cases where exhibitions could be staged, a raised walkway around the top and a gentle descent by half levels to the basement. Shelving of grey-stained ash was complemented by fat, chrome-steel handrails, recessed lighting and board-marked concrete columns. A bronze fascia carried Heffers' new logo, in Stephenson Blake Modern No. 20, lower case, with a colon after the name. Later changes have spoilt the character, but the basics are still in place.

Alan Powers

Queensgate Market

Location: Princess Alexandra
Walk, Huddersfield
Designed by: J. Seymour Harris
Partnership
Opened: 1970
Listed: Grade II

The early 1960s redevelopment of Huddersfield town centre was proposed by Murrayfield Estates, whose architect was commissioned by Huddersfield Corporation to design an integrated replacement market hall on a sloping site.

Project architect Gwyn Roberts and engineer Joe Nicholls of Leonard & Partners took the work of the pioneering Mexico-based architect Félix Candela and inspirational Israeli engineer Eliahu Traum to create novel structures to roof and illuminate the market's 188 stalls. Uniquely, the roof is formed of 21 free-standing, asymmetric, hyperbolic paraboloid concrete shells. The glazing of the 4ft 6in (1.37m) vertical intervals between the shells allows for their movement. Two massive ceramic and steel artworks by Fritz Steller (a student friend of Roberts) celebrate the market's form and function.

Proposed demolition led to its listing in 2005, bringing global attention. The 2022 'Cultural Heart' redevelopment plans of Feilden Clegg Bradley Studios for Kirklees Council preserve the roof shells and art.

Christopher R. Marsden

Indoor Market, Middleton Grange Shopping Centre

Location: Victoria Road, Hartlepool
Designed by: Clifford Culpin & Partners
Opened: 1967–70

The planner Max Lock found that Hartlepool's small shops were struggling, so proposed a single major shopping centre in the heart of Victorian West Hartlepool. It included a new pedestrian high street with to one side an indoor market, replacing a tall red-brick market on Lynn Street. Clifford Culpin was the son of a London county councillor and worked extensively with Labour councils. He and the engineers A. E. Beer & Partners raised the market hall over ground-floor car parking, exploiting a natural fall of the land. The effect of entering the market hall is now more dramatic since the adjoining precinct was roofed over in 1992, enhancing a movement from dark to light created by five enormous rooflights like giant sails – very appropriate for a maritime town. They are formed by a series of cranked reinforced-concrete beams supported on concrete walls lined with small stalls and cafés.

Elain Harwood

Maskreys

Location: Whitchurch Road, Cardiff
Designed by: Powell Alport & Partners
Opened: 1973

Maskreys was an independent furniture retailer founded in Cardiff in 1898. It was a pioneer in importing Scandinavian furniture to the UK and from the 1950s earned a widespread reputation for selling contemporary home furnishings, many with a continental European provenance. When the works to its Whitchurch Road store were completed in 1973, the Aalto-inspired building exemplified the products it showcased. Designed by Gordon Jones of Powell Alport & Partners, the brickwork-faced building had a precast concrete structure spanning the full width of the frameless glazing to the ground floor, while a patent-glazed mansard roof afforded extensive views from the light-filled, top-floor cafeteria.

The business closed in 2011, following the owner's decision to retire, and the building sold. Subsequently, it was unsympathetically converted to a local food store and flats; a stylish piece of early 1970s commercial architecture compromised by not being afforded the protection of listing that it deserved.

Jonathan Vining

THE TWENTIETH CENTURY BOUTIQUE

The twentieth century boutique was a stylish shop, selling clothes or associated goods like perfume and jewellery, clustered in a select set of major cities linked to the fashion industry. Initially small, exclusive and jewel-like, the form of the boutique shifted through the century, as did the kinds of fashion cultures it housed, but it remained the key genre of shop for elite and/or cutting-edge fashion retail.

Whereas other notable historic shop types remain part of the contemporary retail landscape, individual boutique enterprises were often short-lived, their built form ephemeral. Like most small-scale urban shops, boutiques occupied the long, thin ground floor and perhaps first floor of existing shop structures, sandwiched between similar plots, in a patchwork of different styles. The focus and identity of boutique architecture lay in the shopfront and fascia, and interior design, i.e., the elements linked with publicity and display functions. This ordering aligned with that of some other retail formats, but was especially indicative of the boutique, linked so closely as it was with fleeting fashions. Like the clothes, the designs were transient skins, frustrating a more comprehensive architectural approach. Boutiques are best understood as pre-existing buildings dressed and staged by a variety of creative professionals; many culturally important examples did not involve architects and were never published in the architectural press.

This essay looks at three distinct iterations of this shop type, points along the timeline when boutique design chimed closely with temporal consumption cultures: the French-influenced luxury boutiques of the 1920s to the 1950s; the more youthful and informal boutiques of Swinging London of the late 1950s to the 1970s; and the opulent global fashion showcases of the late twentieth century. The geographies of high and avant-garde fashion through the twentieth century were primarily metropolitan, so the British boutique story is largely about London, with echoes in other major cities. The international perspective tells of interwar Parisian couture boutiques, then replicated in the most fashionable districts of other Western capitals; a post-war 'Swinging London' moment; and a late twentieth century resurgence of flagship stores for global high fashion brands. In London, key examples clustered around stylish shopping streets, initially Bond Street in Mayfair, moving to the King's Road and Carnaby Street, then Knightsbridge and Kensington, before recentring in Mayfair and Covent Garden.

While small-scale fashionable shops were not new, boutiques emerged as a significant and distinct retail genre, with an identifiable built form, during the 1920s. Paris was the world's undisputed fashion capital, and these gem-like stores evoked French high fashion, modelled on the new retail and showroom spaces being developed in French couturiers' salons. Early couturier boutiques by

RIGHT Ernö Goldfinger's shop for Helena Rubinstein, Grafton Street, London, 1935

fashion designer Sonia Delauney and architects Robert Mallet-Stevens and René Herbst in 1920s Paris were soon copied by Chanel, Schiaparelli and most leading French fashion houses. It was significant that these couturier boutiques were frequently architect-designed, which had not previously been common for either couture houses or small specialist shops. Couturiers' international clientele, coupled with published volumes of new boutique designs, facilitated the boutique's spread to the exclusive shopping streets of other cities, notably Berlin, Stuttgart, Rotterdam and Prague. London, of course, had its own fashion designers, and opened a range of what, in January 1950, *Vogue* deemed 'entrancing little shops'. Gerald Lacoste's glamorous mirrored and draped interiors for Norman Hartnell in Bruton Street fell into this category.

The boutique format and styles were swiftly adopted by a range of other luxury fashion shops: high-end dress shops, sometimes called 'madam shops', milliners, perfumiers and jewellers. See, for example, Ernö Goldfinger for Helena Rubinstein in Grafton Street. In a period of economic and geopolitical instability, the boutique proved a useful business strategy for propping up high-end fashion design and luxury retail. Small and easily convertible, boutique projects were cheap and low-risk compared with the high-stakes building projects of large department stores or families of chain stores.

Early boutique owners commissioned modernist/moderne styles, precisely because they communicated the modernity of the goods sold. They drew on department and chain store architectural display and communication strategies in approaches to their façade, window and interior designs. But the boutique's design vocabulary was subtly different from its more affordable contemporaries. It was an architecture of glass, polished metal and elegant interiors. For example, *Vogue* described Molyneux's 'Cool grey walls, crisp cut chandeliers, and air of quiet restraint'. Yet, fashion retail's association with the novelty, desire and femininity clearly troubled some parts of the architectural establishment. Herbert Tayler wrote in *The Architectural Review* for February 1957 that 'shops are never great architecture … they are a minor architectural art, capricious, mutable, transient, evanescent.'

Prominent architects did, though, accept the available work, and must surely have been attracted by the measure of experimentation allowed by boutique design. See, for example, the intricate neon work on Vincent Harris's 1926 shop for perfumier Atkinsons, and Serge Chermayeff's elegant floating showcases in his 1938 store for the jeweller Ciro, both in Old Bond Street.

By the 1950s, the boutique's favoured architectural style of contemporary modern was well matched with the tasteful, if often conservative, garments sold, while

LEFT One of the changing façades of Granny Takes a Trip, featuring a 1948 Dodge saloon car, Nigel Waymouth, 1968 also displaying stylistic similarities with chain stores. Department stores were now opening in-store 'boutiques', primarily in an attempt to reinvigorate lacklustre in-house fashion offers. With the dilution of the boutique's exclusivity, what had been novel and cutting edge had become passé. Small, elegant shops in historically exclusive streets continued to be designed and redesigned, but they were no longer the most fashionable shops in town.

On the eve of the Swinging Sixties, the boutique baton was passed from Paris to London, reflecting a significant shift in the kind of fashion businesses commissioning their designs. *Domus* noted that 'Britain is known the world over for ... the boutiques drowned in the sound of the Beat'. London's most noteworthy fashion retail clusters were moving from historic Bond Street in Mayfair to the former backwaters of Carnaby Street in Soho and the King's Road in Chelsea, before colonising parts of Kensington, mapped in *Get Dressed: A Useful Guide to London's Boutiques*. These were places where a new, younger generation of designers and entrepreneurs could access cheaper rents and shorter leases.

In 1955, when designer-entrepreneur Mary Quant's Bazaar opened on the King's Road, then John Stephen's His Clothes near Carnaby Street, they were at the forefront of a new youthful and confident fashion culture that rejected social and cultural conventions; social hubs as much as shops.

The new boutiques were initially styled with the same simple modernity as the upmarket chain store, see for example Conran Design Group's design for Mary Quant's next Bazaar in Brompton Road, Knightsbridge of 1959. But, increasingly, boutique architecture was playful and rebellious, eclectic and even makeshift, and it was these subsequent examples that came to represent the boutiques of Swinging London in the popular imagination.

New boutique designs were worlds away from the contemporaneous 'architecture-as-planning' of the new shopping centres and took little note of the retail design guides of the 1950s, with their promotion of airy, modern spaces and careful scientific studies of light refraction and footfall patterns. The well-trodden ground of 'retail architecture as advertisement' was being used in new, often shocking ways. *Design* wrote about what it termed the 'Carnaby Street approach': 'the increased freedom and spending power of the young are behind the movement away from dowdy good taste and over-seriousness.' Garnett, Cloughley, Blakemore's Just Looking on the King's Road exemplified these approaches to the façade, designed to 'dramatise and call attention to itself with circular forms and reflecting surfaces.'

These boutique businesses took leases in decaying old shops in cheaper streets, again employing a design approach of surface and skim. *Domus* found, 'creativity and

RIGHT David Chipperfield store for Issey Miyake, Sloane Street, London, 1985

invention may begin at any moment without there being any need to destroy anything, and that they can be spread over any terrain like a coat of paint'. *Design* magazine was more scathing, 'Carnaby Street is stuffed with original and influential ideas, but they are often tattily carried out'.

Materials like fibreglass, plastics and colourful paint became commonplace, although the stores were stylistically diverse. Some stores like Just Looking exemplified a space-age, futuristic-pop fusion. Others were nostalgic and historicist, epitomised by Barbara Hulanicki's Biba, which opened in Abingdon Road, Kensington in 1964, and successive Biba stores, whose design, branding and clothes referenced Art Nouveau and Art Deco. Often dark, seductive interiors were paired with lively, chaotic, surreal window displays and 'pop' signage.

The store designs were just as likely to be the work of a range of different types of designers as architects, often drawing on young talent that operated in the same circles as the fashion designers. The World's End area of the King's Road was a key site for this, for example artist-poster designer-entrepreneur Nigel Waymouth's swiftly changing shopfronts for Granny Takes a Trip on the King's Road, including a 1968 version, featuring a brightly painted sawn-off 1940s car. The reliance on artists concorded with an increasingly conceptual approach to fashion and the shop environment. Vivienne Westwood wrote of her King's Road boutiques, 'this wasn't fashion as a commodity, this was fashion as an idea', casting light on exactly why the revolutionary boutiques of this era required a new design approach.

Successful shop design has always worked symbiotically with the goods sold, but this wasn't fashion retail, or retail architecture, as they had previously been practised. By the end of the period, for many it was '[making] a mockery of what is known as modern architecture and good design. For those who set their standards of taste by principles, there is no sense in it.' The upsetting of architectural conventions and the deliberately ephemeral aesthetic was bewildering, as expressed by José Manser: 'The few remaining Edwardian and thirties shops are going and now they are being replaced by cheap marine-ply and paint façades, their interiors often either brash or plastic or barely furnished at all'. Yet it was these ephemeral, barely architectural, boutiques of Swinging London that became one of the few retail innovations that Britain exported.

The radical boutique had largely run its course by the early 1970s, with many designers moving into the mainstream (e.g., Quant's Ginger Group). That said, Vivienne Westwood, part of the next wave of rebel fashion designers, was still able to use boutiques to provoke scandal on the King's Road, opening Let it Rock in 1971 (with Malcolm McLaren), followed swiftly by Too Fast to Live Too Young to Die, SEX and others. Even more shocking

LEFT Katherine Hamnett shop, Norman Foster, Knightsbridge, London, 1989

than her predecessors, her clothes and store environments left a lasting legacy in British fashion.

From the 1980s, boutiques began to shed their associations with radical youth fashion, and again became the preserve of luxury designer fashion. The locus switched from Swinging London to a more grown-up range of fashion's world cities. New York was especially influential, from Architectural League/Minetta Brook for Comme des Garçons in 1982, to Rem Koolhaas's SoHo Epicenter for Prada, opened in 2001, and Frank Gehry's shop in Tribeca for Issey Miyake in 2000.

Since the era of 1920s couturier, boutique global branding practices had transformed high fashion, reflected in the design and planning of boutiques. The new incarnation of the boutique was essentially an elite, limited-edition chain store, while invoking an older 'boutique' identity through its close associations with exclusivity and cutting-edge fashion. Access to big budgets now allowed for the involvement of star architects, while both architect and fashion house had a well-honed style, melded together on each project. Designs were coherent and precisely detailed, originating in high-tech and post-industrial architecture.

London had a key role within this, with a cluster of prominent high-tech 1980s stores, such as Norman Foster's 1986 whiteout store for Katharine Hamnett in the Brompton Road, its clothes racks dwarfed within a cavernous former workshop space. Eva Jiřičná's work for Joseph was equally significant; in 1989 *The Architectural Review* described her approach as: 'the austere, elegant idiom of black and off-white punctuated by moments of silver High Tech detailing'. Her stores for Joseph in Chelsea and on Fulham Road are two key examples. Armstrong Chipperfield with Greaves-Lord offered a more joyous and colourful version of the boutique for Issey Miyake in Sloane Street. By the late twentieth century, tastes had edged towards luxury, minimalist modern, epitomised by John Pawson for Jigsaw in 1996.

The boutique's trajectory through the twentieth century reached its end point with the more corporate super-boutiques of a new generation of international fashion brands like Prada, LVMH and Gucci Group in the 2000s. These showy new flagships were no longer typically small, but were still essentially an architecture of shopfront and interior, of surface and display. Taken together, the boutiques of the successive waves offer an eclectic celebration of the century's fashionable architectures, clothes and commodities. The roles played by surface and fashionable items meant their designs represented a challenge to many. But it was barely worth objecting: each boutique slipped for a while into the footprint of existing shops, leaving the older architectures above intact, only to be replaced a few years on. Blink and you missed it.

Bronwen Edwards

Wartski

Location: 14 Grafton Street, London
Designed by: John Bruckland
Opened: 1974
Listed: Grade II

Wartski captures a particular trend in post-war shop front design, defined by a materials-led approach, assertive massing and the shop window relegated to a bit player. John Bruckland's bold, rectilinear composition uses materials to maximum effect: bronze, white marble and black polished granite, with elegant flashes of gold. The result speaks to the luxury and bespoke nature of what lies within.

Wartski specialises in antique jewellery and works by Carl Fabergé. The company was founded in 1865 in Bangor, North Wales by Morris Wartski, a Russian Jewish émigré, before moving to Llandudno in 1907 and opening a London branch in 1911. The Grafton Street store, within a granite-clad block by Richard Seifert and Partners was their second London store.

Bruckland was an architect specialising in interior and exhibition design. The shop front was listed in 2012 and is set to be incorporated in a redevelopment of Seifert's building; Wartski moved to St James's Street in 2018.

Posy Metz

195

21. NORTHUMBERLAND STREET, NEWCASTLE-ON-TYNE.

Former British Home Stores, Newcastle upon Tyne

Location: 72–74 Northumberland Street, Newcastle upon Tyne
Designed by: North & Robin; murals by Henry and Joyce Collins
Opened: 1974

This store was developed for C&A and is now occupied by Primark, but is remarkable for a mural installed for British Home Stores (BHS). Henry and Joyce (née Pallot) Collins designed murals across the country, first for Sainsbury's and then for BHS, that featured elements of local history. They researched each location, drawing on local industries and economies as well as history, geography and architecture. Here a series of concrete reliefs depict Newcastle through the ages: bridges and boats are prominent, and the predominant colour is blue, foregrounding the importance of shipbuilding and the Tyne. Vibrant areas of mosaic catch the passing shopper's eye. Close up, richly textured concrete creates visual depth and invites tactile exploration. Letters conveying historic names and dates are incorporated alongside recognisable figures, symbols and places, from a Geordie miner to ancient gods. Bronze paint (now badly faded) highlights small sections of the reliefs, including Hadrian, profiled on a coin.

Natalie Bradbury

MONKCHESTER

COLLIER
BRIG
1704-1880

OCE ANVS

AVGVSTVS

Irvine Centre

Location: Irvine, North Ayrshire
Designed by: David Gosling with
Barry Maitland, Irvine
Development Corporation
Opened: 1975

The Irvine Centre stands as a swan song to megastructural thinking. Evoking the contrived urbanity of the floating concrete deck planned for Hook, Hampshire, but never built, the Centre springs out over the low-lying River Irvine, its indoor shopping 'street' continuing, in mid-air, the pedestrianised historic burgh onto which it was grafted. Hallmarks of the Metabolists abound, from the linear service 'spine' and 'rib ducts' above the shopping concourse, to the circulatory system of roads and plant rooms below. Dead ends sprout from its strong geometries, a nod to the determined extensibility of Cumbernauld Town Centre.

Only from the riverbanks does the building's scale become apparent. Bursting forth from the burgh's high ground, the megastructure soars over river and roads with all the thrust and swagger that defined these experimental leviathans. Though unfinished and a little ragged, the Irvine Centre still harnesses something of those post-war reveries of a space age utopia.

Joss Durnan

Cofferidge Close

Location: High Street, Stony
Stratford, Milton Keynes
Designed by: Milton Keynes
Development Corporation
Opened: 1976

Praised at the time for 'achieving a balance of old and new', Cofferidge Close helped alleviate the struggles of the small, market town of Stony Stratford. The development was part of the Milton Keynes Development Corporation's initiative to assimilate the old settlement into the new town with sensitivity. With its red brick frontage spanning over 100ft (30m) along the High Street and its carved, painted signs, Cofferidge Close leans into Stony Stratford's existing fabric – see, for example, the hanging signs outside the nearby Cock Inn and Bull Hotel. Yet, be under no illusion that this development – led by architect Derek Walker – is a pastiche homage to bygone times. The colonnades facing onto the High Street are defiantly modern; the painted signs, meanwhile, are by Malcolm Fowler's Shirt Sleeve Studio, known for their work with Tate Britain, and for bringing a touch of the 'King's Road taste' to this market town.

Ellen Brown

Quadrant Centre

Location: Nelson Street, Swansea
Designed by: Building Design Partnership
Opened: 1978

Fifteen years after the opening of the UK's first indoor shopping centre in Birmingham, Swansea joined the new era of retail design with its Quadrant Centre, located south of the central market. It is a large complex of arcaded shops with an anchor department store building, bus station and multi-storey car park, all skilfully fitted into the site. The configuration in plan of four double-height malls radiating from a lofty central space is legible and provides good pedestrian linkages to much of the surrounding urban grain. The principal space, Central Square, is the most dramatic visually with its tubular-steel, space-frame roof structure and sloping clerestory glazing, and offers vistas along each of the malls. Covered shopping centres of the period may not be particularly well regarded now as a building type, but this is a good example that is robust enough to adapt as part of emerging city centre regeneration proposals.

Jonathan Vining

ASDA Supermarket

Location: South Woodham
Ferrers, Essex
Designed by: Holder & Mathias
Opened: 1978

Essex County Council regulated South Woodham Ferrers, the first new town designed using the 1973 *Essex Design Guide*, to look like a traditional Essex market town. Holder and Mathias's solution to integrating a superstore was to embrace its scale and horizontal emphasis and give it the character of a large tithe barn with an off-centre midstrey denoting the entrance.

The aesthetic gained authenticity through high-quality materials including handmade clay bricks, plain tiles and weatherboarding. A second midstrey was added in 1985 when the store was extended. The massing to the north was disguised as a series of gabled roofs, giving the impression of smaller historic buildings addressing a traditional market square. The clock tower was raised in 1985 to mark the new town centre. Inside, the sloping roofs were intended to look like a Victorian market hall. Derided by some, the tithe-barn aesthetic became an influential template for superstores and retail parks.

Nicholas Page

Arndale Centre, Manchester

Location: Market Street, Manchester
Designed by: Ken Shone, for Wilson Womersley
Opened: 1979

Manchester's Arndale Centre was the largest constructed in the UK. Its original buff yellow tiled mass was built in phases between 1972 and 1979, financed by a public-private partnership. The Corporation needed developers' capital to realise their post-war reconstruction and in 1967 dedicated the Market Street Comprehensive Development Area to enable the project. The Arndale was synonymous with the rise in consumerism and reflected the planning zeitgeist for separating pedestrians and traffic. Despite the local authority and architect wanting a sequence of open spaces, the Centre was inward-looking and enclosed, containing covered malls, squares and a market, as well as a bus station, multi-storey car park and offices. This immersive experience was controlled and provided a glamorous theatrical counterpoint to the rest of the city. The seemingly endless interior housed a roll call of British retailers – C&A, British Home Stores, W. H. Smith, Mothercare, Dolcis, Beaverbrooks, Thorntons and Timpson – set amid terrazzo, chrome and aluminium-clad surfaces.

Richard Brook

Shopping Building (The Centre:MK)

Location: Midsummer Boulevard, Milton Keynes
Designed by: Christopher Woodward, Milton Keynes Development Corporation Architect's Department
Opened: 1979
Listed: Grade II

The Shopping Building is naturally lit, inspired by Milan's Galleria Vittorio Emanuele II and mirror glass buildings seen by Christopher Woodward in Los Angeles. Its greatest conceit is that it is serviced from the roof via a road bridge carried over the building, removing the need for basement servicing. But it is the travertine that paves the interiors that give the Shopping Building its civic elegance.

Conceived more as two covered high streets than a cathedral of consumption, it is ageing gracefully; in the summer, the trees that line the 2,100ft (650m) arcades now create a luscious reflection in the building's mirrored glass. Artworks include Liliane Lijn's *Circle of Light*, commissioned in 1977. The Shopping Building always seems to be threatened by a new scheme by the centre's owners to make it more shoppable: some planters have gone, and the open square remodelled for restaurants. But on the whole, it has held its own.

Ellen Brown

1980
onwards

Wood Green
Shopping City

Location: Haringey, London
Designed by: Sheppard Robson
Opened: 1981

Travelling northwards through low-rise Victorian suburbia, it is a shock to come upon the massive scale of Shopping City, which looms into view, a vast red-brick colossus. It rises up on both sides of the road, the two parts linked by a bridge. The first floor is cantilevered out to create an arcade at street level, increasing the feeling of passing through a canyon. Shopping City is a megastructural mélange, using three million Southwater bricks, over a 14 acre (5.7 ha) site, to house 500,000 sq. ft (46,450 sq. m) of shopping space, a 70-stall market hall, car parking for 1,500 cars and, on top of it all, an incongruous village of 201 pitched-roofed houses and flats. It contrasts with both the inward-looking box mall of nearby Brent Cross, and the picturesque postmodernism of Ealing Broadway Centre, in that it uses a modernist aesthetic to exploit the dramatic potential and sheer ferocious thrill of a really big project.

Otto Saumarez Smith

St David's Shopping Centre

Location: Cardiff
Architect: Vernon W. Crofts,
J. Seymour Harris Partnership
Opened: 1982

St David's Centre, 'the shape of shopping for the future', provided a retail focus for the city's ambitious redevelopment envisaged in the Buchanan Plan of 1964. The only outcome of what became Centreplan 70, it reflected the fashion for indoor shopping centres but owed something too to the city's historic arcades.

As the centre was formed by the individual fronts of anchor stores, many pre-dating the development, it is experienced only from the inside. Well-lit and airy, combining extensive planting with postmodernist geometrical design, it creates a comfortable but energizing space to shop and rest. It was extended in 2009. A life-size bronze of Gareth Edwards was all that was needed to say 'This is Wales'.

An external architectural statement is made by the St David's National Concert Hall, also by Seymour Harris. Technically an addition to the shopping centre, together they reflect the high quality, civic approach envisioned by the city council.

Lindsay Christian

Cameron Toll Shopping Centre

Location: Lady Road, Edinburgh
Designed by: Michael Laird Architects
Opened: 1984

One of Scotland's first major 'out-of-town' shopping centres, on Edinburgh's south side, Cameron Toll had 38 stores, originally including a Sainsbury's SavaCentre hypermarket. Plans, drawn up in the mid-1970s, were constrained by nearby houses and a walkway required along Braid Burn. Car parks were to be carefully landscaped. The sensitive site and Sainsbury's policy of quality architectural patronage may explain the choice of a major Edinburgh practice.

The building is wrapped in a glazed skin, angled largely towards the sky to minimise its bulk through reflections. Behind it is a service void, backed by a dark-painted blockwork wall. At night, lighting in the void created interest. The shopping arcade itself is day-lit, and originally featured a bespoke lighting treatment as well as lush planting. Despite being built to serve drivers, the centre connects reasonably well with the surrounding area. It shows how this typology can rise above the banal.

Alistair Fair

Princes Square

Location: Glasgow
Designed by: Hugh Martin
and Partners
Opened: 1988

Princes Square started life in the 1840s as business chambers designed by John Baird for Sir James Campbell, Lord Provost of Glasgow. The block of handsome sandstone buildings provided good 'bones' for a Covent Garden-esque redevelopment, pitched as Scotland's first speciality shopping centre. A vaulted, glazed roof was added to the internal courtyard, and elegant staircases, criss-crossing escalators and open lifts provided access to balconied galleries, inspired by the Bradbury Building in Los Angeles (Sumner Hunt, 1893). The tubular supporting structure was designed to draw the eye upwards. Decoration adorned almost every surface, including etched glass on the lifts by Maria McClafferty, Art Nouveau-inspired ironwork by Alan Dawson and Charles Henshaw, floor mosaic by Jane Muir, stained glass by John Clark and a *trompe l'oeil* mural of famous Glaswegians by Dai Vaughan. The elevation facing Buchanan Street featured a sculpture of a peacock, hinting towards the eclectically styled interior.

Grace Etherington

Sainsbury's, Camden Town

Location: 17–21 Camden Road, London
Designed by: Nicholas Grimshaw
and Partners
Opened: 1988
Listed: Grade II

The first purpose-built supermarket to be listed, this 'unapologetically futuristic' building drew extreme responses: artist Frank Auerbach saw it as a building of 'real power and intelligent character', while novelist Beryl Bainbridge expressed distaste. The immense metallic carapace extends along much of an entire block, taking in Canal Walk, an ingenious housing scheme facing onto the Grand Union Canal. Nicholas Grimshaw returned to the aesthetic of the railway station for what is essentially a massive, steel-framed shed. Sainsbury's specified their usual open-plan shop floor, here of great depth. The two side extensions add impact – a pair of book ends expressed as the terrace of houses and on the front elevation. Here, clad in aluminium, they cantilever out to provide first floor office units. The integration of different functions and the multiple faces of surrounding street buildings is the masterstroke in this commanding building. I admire it as much today as I did 35 years ago.

Gillian Darley

St Enoch Centre, Glasgow

Location: St Enoch Square, Glasgow
Designed by: Reiach & Hall with
Gollins Melvin Ward Partnership
Opened: 1989

After the Victorian St Enoch Station closed in 1966, the Scottish Development Agency acquired its site, parallel to Argyle Street. They published proposals for a shopping centre in 1982 after a previous mixed-use scheme fell through. It was developed with Sears and the Church of England commissioners in a public/private partnership, at a cost of £160 million.

Dubbed 'the Glasgow greenhouse', it was the largest glazed structure in Europe upon completion – more roof than wall, butted against its own multi-storey car park. Energy-saving was a key design consideration: the arcade is wholly day-lit and uses solar gain beneficially. As originally configured, it included an ice rink, as well as shops and cafés.

It formed part of a determined campaign to rebrand Glasgow as a leisure and shopping destination. Subsequently remodelled, in 2022 there are proposals to demolish the building in order to create a new landscape of buildings and open streets.

Alistair Fair

The Italian Centre

Location: 7 John Street, Glasgow
Designed by: Page & Park
Opened: 1990

The Italian Centre was an early commission for local architects Page & Park, and combined high-end shops with a restaurant, café, flats and offices set around a cosmopolitan courtyard. The façades of existing nineteenth-century tenements were retained, and the idea of the Glaswegian back court, typically cluttered with rubbish bins, was completely reimagined and filled with contemporary sculpture and a sleek, narrow canal. Covered walkways were modelled on porticoes in Bologna, glazed courtyard canopies and figurative sculptures by Jack Sloan had a distinctly futurist feel, and luxury shops, including Armani and Versace, transported visitors to Milan. Rome was represented by an arcaded extension on John Street and neo-classical sculptures depicting *Italia* and *Mercury* by Alexander Stoddart. The project won several awards, with the abundance of sculpture being particularly well received, and it was described by historian and broadcaster Dan Cruickshank as a reminder that 'great things are still possible'.

Grace Etherington

22 Shad Thames

Location: 22 Shad Thames, London
Designed by: Michael & Patty Hopkins;
structural engineer Buro Happold
Opened: 1991
Listed: Grade II

David Mellor commissioned a flexible building providing a showroom, workshop, offices and family home, on the site of a nineteenth-century warehouse in London's docklands, then being regenerated. The design of the six-storey building, which has an in-situ concrete frame clad with glass, steel and lead, was influenced by the architects' recent visit to Louis Kahn's Yale Center for British Art in New Haven, Connecticut, while the meticulous concrete finishes reflect the work of Tadao Ando. Mellor and his workforce were closely involved; Patty Hopkins said that he 'applied the same degree of care to the hand sanding of the internal concrete columns as he did to burnishing his beautiful cutlery.'

When Mellor left in 1996, designer Sir Terence Conran took over the building as the headquarters of Conran and Partners, briefly living in the duplex penthouse flat. After the company departed in 2020, threatened redevelopment caused the C20 Society to seek its listing.

Susannah Charlton

IKEA Croydon

Location: Valley Retail Park,
Purley Way, Croydon
Designed by: SRA Architects
Opened: 1992

IKEA was founded in Sweden by Ingvar Kamprad in 1943 and opened its first UK store in Warrington in 1987. The blue box of the Croydon branch stands next to two 300ft (90m) high brick chimneys, topped with blue and yellow striped branding. A local landmark, they are all that remains of Croydon B power station, designed by Robert Atkinson (1946; demolished 1991).

IKEA changed the experience as well as the market for furniture shopping, previously dominated by retail park giants like MFI. It has a deliberately distinctive typology: the blue box; the one-way serpentine route through mocked-up rooms in the store; the canteen serving meatballs; and the self-service stacks. Look at any rental property listing, and the photos will likely feature a Lack table or a Billy bookcase. Though the flatpack names are parodied as much as getting lost in the store, IKEA furniture remains ubiquitous in the contemporary home.

Katrina Navickas

Turquoise Island Florist's Kiosk

Location: Wild at Heart, 222 Westbourne Grove, London
Designed by: CZWG
Opened: 1993

Only in Notting Hill could delphinium bouquets bedeck the glossy prow of a PoMo public convenience. How it looks is largely down to the determination of a local resident, the late John Scott of the Pembridge Association, who approached Piers Gough of CZWG to design it. The florists' kiosk was added to the brief after Scott argued that the rental income would offset the running costs of the loos.

Turquoise Island, as it's known, is a triangular pavilion oversailed by a glazed canopy like Guimard's Paris Metro entrances. Its blue-green glazed bricks, specially made by Shaws of Darwen, were deemed far too enjoyable to be confined to the lavatory interiors. Their colour, according to Gough, 'seemed suitable for this rather raffish area of London'. Turquoise Island was the original location of Wild at Heart, the luxury florist founded by Nikki Tibbles, and three decades on Londoners are still spending pennies there.

Geraint Franklin

Jigsaw

Location: 126–7 New
Bond Street, London
Designed by: John Pawson
Opened: 1996

The minimal elegance of this space required nerve to enter, its formal clarity packing a punch on New Bond Street. As his publicity material admitted, John Pawson had drawn 'on earlier gallery designs'. The immaculate concrete finishes and plainspoken elements, such as the huge clear glazed frontage and uncompromising stair, smacked of Japan where Jigsaw had opened a store that year. The fenestration, in two parts each quartered by black glazing bars, announced the double-height entrance space, before pointing customers to the rear of the store or downwards. Where clothes were displayed, the areas were nudged into life with lighting and translucent screens. It was a wonderful place to be but did not last: by 2012 it was vacant. Now a luxury goods shop, elements of the stair survive but little else. Of Pawson's uncompromising vision there is no trace. The febrile retail world never looks over its shoulder.

Gillian Darley

Siop Menter

Location: Garreg,
Llanfrothen, Gwynedd
Designed by: David Lea
Opened: 1998

David Lea was an architect of principle who throughout his career sought to design beautiful, low-impact buildings that were in harmony with the natural world. Near his home in Snowdonia, he designed such a building for a community co-operative society, Menter Llanfrothen, that originally housed shops, a post office, petrol station and workshops for rent. Long and low, so that it did not interrupt the view of the homes opposite, it has a low-energy construction (predominantly in timber) with a regular structural grid for subdivision and flexibility for future adaptation.

Like many of his buildings it is day-lit from overhead and has a wonderful quality of natural light. Although the building is now somewhat altered, the robustness of the design concept is still evident, even if the formerly exposed structural timber frame has been unsympathetically lined with plastic. Its value to the community endures as a vibrant local café and shop.

Jonathan Vining

Selfridges

Location: The Bull Ring, Birmingham
Designed by: Future Systems;
structural engineers, Arup
Opened: 2003

The 1960s Bull Ring Shopping Centre was redeveloped in 2000–3 with an open pedestrian street and some individual buildings, of which this is the award winner. Its waveform shape made it immediately iconic, a 'blobitecture' earning the name 'Digbeth Dalek'. It is clad in 15,000 anodised aluminium discs supported on individual bolts cast into a blue wrapper of sprayed concrete that conceals a steel frame. Jan Kaplický gave his source as a Paco Rabanne dress. The elevations have few openings: undulating shop windows at street level outlined in yellow glazing, and face-like openings on the rounded corner, one belching a glass walkway.

The interior is important too, glittering yet also claustrophobic – impressing the urgency to shop. Ascending, the designers were Future Systems (who also brought cohesion with the escalators), Eldridge Smerin, Stanton Williams and Cibic & Partners with Lees Associates for the top-floor café, pale with glass fittings and big roof slats.

Katriona Byrne

Liverpool ONE

Location: 5 Wall Street, Liverpool
Planned by: Building Design
Partnership (BDP)
Opened: 2008

After Liverpool's blitzed ruins were carted for landfill in Crosby much of the city was a giant car park. There was an opportunity for a fresh start, but an ambitious scheme by architect-planner Graeme Shankland in the 1960s was only partially implemented.

Instead, BDP produced a new plan, respecting the historic street pattern and seamlessly linking the old core to the waterfront so it is hard to say where their development begins and where it ends. BDP also produced some, but not all of the buildings. Construction began in 2004. It is a collection by 26 notable designers, including FAT, CZWG, WilkinsonEyre and Haworth Tompkins. Together they make a post-modern collage at the scale of the urban block. Street furniture, pavilions and art works add colour, pattern and wit. The result is a triumph of townscape, that unfolds like a film, with views to the waterfront and glimpses of the Liver Building.

Andrew Crompton

Waitrose, Truro

Location: Tregurra Park, Truro
Designed by: Ben Pentreath
Opened: 2016

Cornwall Council decreed a park-and-ride scheme in this valley east of Truro, which required land belonging to the Duchy of Cornwall estates. They reluctantly agreed and their scheme includes new housing and premises for Waitrose, combined with the Great Cornish Food Store, an indoor farmers' market.

Ben Pentreath has designed a number of larger development projects for the Duchy since his first work at Poundbury in the 1990s. Here, a Royal Crescent, with something of the audacious grandeur and open outlook of the John Wood the Younger's Bath masterpiece, looks down from the crest of the hill, and below this Waitrose fits into the southern slope. While supermarkets have previously taken on vernacular disguises, this is the first to sport a Doric portico, in this case with columns of solid Cornish granite. As the designer explains, 'the temple front was in my mind because it's the building where the middle classes go to worship daily.'

Alan Powers

Coal Drops Yard

Location: York Way, Camden, London
Designed by: Heatherwick Studio
Opened: 2018
Listed: The original Eastern Coal Drops at King's Cross Goods Yard is listed at Grade II

Designed as a focal point for the massive redevelopment of the industrial land behind King's Cross station, this glamorous shopping centre extends and joins together two Victorian 'coal drops' – structures to receive and store coal arriving by train for onward distribution by barge and cart. There is 100,000 sq. ft (9,230 sq. m) of new retail space in total, with shop units varying from 160 sq. ft (15 sq. m) to over 20,000 sq. ft (1,900 sq. m).

Designer Thomas Heatherwick said that he set out to make 'an amazing place', and that 'the shopping is the excuse for a place'. It is deliberately flamboyant and, with interlocking pedestrian routes at different levels, sets out to encourage interaction. 'To be with your fellow humans is more precious than ever. You don't have to go out. So somewhere has to mean something and not be generic duplicate, which you may have got away with 20 or 30 years ago before the digital revolution.'

Catherine Croft

ACKNOWLEDGEMENTS

C20 Society would like to thank all those who have contributed entries or photographs to this book, or have shared their knowledge during its gestation. Particular thanks go to John East for taking so many new photographs for the book.

Josh Abbott printer, runs the Modernism in Metro-land website and tours, author of *A Guide to Modernism in Metro-land*

Natalie Bradbury writer and researcher interested in public art and education

Ellen Brown writer and PhD student at the University of Warwick, researching post-war shopping centre architecture

Timothy Brittain-Catlin is an architectural historian and teacher at the University of Cambridge

Richard Brook architect, architectural historian and Professor of Architecture at Lancaster University

Katriona Byrne senior lecturer and course director of MA Conservation of the Historic Environment at Birmingham City University

Susannah Charlton consultant and editor, architectural and garden heritage

Lindsay Christian Heritage Management Officer at Monmouthshire County Council and secretary of C20 Cymru

Emily Cole senior architectural investigator with Historic England, author of *Stevenage: Pioneering New Town Centre*

Catherine Croft director of the Twentieth Century Society

Andrew Crompton architectural historian and Reader at Liverpool School of Architecture

Gillian Darley historian, journalist and former president of the Twentieth Century Society

Robert Dowden member of the Twentieth Century Society and committee member of C20 South West group

Joss Durnan archaeologist and architectural historian, Senior Ancient Monuments Officer at Historic Environment Scotland

John East interim local authority management and regeneration professional. Unofficial photographer for the Twentieth Century Society

Bronwen Edwards senior lecturer in geography and town planning at Leeds Beckett University, a specialist in feminist, cultural and historical geography & architectural history

Grace Etherington former caseworker for Twentieth Century Society, PhD student at University of Edinburgh

Alistair Fair Reader in Architectural History, University of Edinburgh

Susan Fielding Senior Investigator (Historic Buildings), Royal Commission on the Ancient and Historical Monuments of Wales, chair of C20 Cymru

Geraint Franklin historian with Historic England and author of *John Outram* in the Twentieth Century Architects series

Miles Glendinning Professor of Architectural Conservation at the University of Edinburgh, specialist in the global history of mass housing

Tom Goodwin volunteer with the Twentieth Century Society, assistant heritage consultant at Purcell

Mark Hazell publican, member of the Twentieth Century Society

Elain Harwood senior architectural investigator with Historic England, author and co-editor of the Twentieth Century Society Journal

Andrew Jackson architectural historian, trustee and national groups coordinator for the Twentieth Century Society

Christopher R. Marsden architectural history and public art researcher

Euan McCulloch Docomomo Scotland committee member and caseworker for Architectural Heritage Society of Scotland. Lawyer with long-standing interest in C20th architecture.

Posy Metz senior listing adviser with Historic England

Catherine Moriarty writer and curator

Kathryn A. Morrison architectural historian, author of *English Shops & Shopping: An Architectural History*

Katrina Navickas professor of history at the University of Hertfordshire

Nicholas Page Principal Heritage Advisor, Enfield Council, previously heritage consultant for Place Services (ECC)

Lynn Pearson architectural historian, author of *England's Co-operative Movement: An Architectural History*

Kenneth Powell architectural critic, consultant and historian

Alan Powers trustee and former chairman of the Twentieth Century Society, specialist in twentieth-century British art and design

Jo Prinsen consultant historical researcher and dalle-de-verre expert

Peter Ruback trustee and former chairman of the Twentieth Century Society, involved in planning and conservation in central London

Otto Saumarez Smith trustee and chair of casework committee of the Twentieth Century Society, associate professor at University of Warwick

Aidan Turner-Bishop former librarian and chair of the C20 North West group

Jonathan Vining practising architect and urban designer, trustee of the Dewi-Prys Thomas Trust and commissioner of the Royal Commission on the Ancient and Historical Monuments of Wales.

Sarah Walford teaching fellow at University of Warwick

Finn Walsh built environment communications consultant

Matthew Whitfield architectural investigator at Historic England

Coco Whittaker senior caseworker for the Twentieth Century Society

FURTHER READING

Josh Abbott, *A Guide to Modernism in Metro-land*, London, Unbound, 2020

Neil Bingham, *The New Boutique: Fashion and Design*, London, Merrell, 2005

Rachel Bowlby, *Back to the Shops*, Oxford, Oxford University Press, 2022

C. Breward et al, eds., *Swinging Sixties: Fashion in London and Beyond 1955–1970*, London, V & A Publishing, 2006

Emily Cole, *Stevenage: Pioneering New Town Centre*, London, Historic England, 2021

Susannah Charlton & Elain Harwood, eds., *100 Buildings 100 Years*, London, Batsford, 2014

Gillian Darley, *Excellent Essex*, London, Old Street Publishing, 2019

Clare Dowdy, *One Off: Independent Retail Design*, London, Laurence King, 2008

Tara Draper-Stumm, *London Shops: The World's Emporium*, London, English Heritage, 2003

Arthur Trystan Edwards, *The Architecture of Shops*, London, Chapman & Hall, 1933

Bronwen Edwards, 'Swinging Boutiques and the Modern Store: Designing Shops for Post-War London', London Journal, 2006

Marnie Fogg, *Boutique: A '60s Cultural Phenomenon*, London, Mitchell Beazley, 2003

Geraint Franklin & Elain Harwood, *Post-Modern Buildings in Britain*, London, Batsford, 2017

Elain Harwood, *Brutalist Britain*, London, Batsford, 2022

Elain Harwood, *Mid-Century Modern*, London, Batsford, 2021

Elain Harwood, *Art Deco Britain*, London, Batsford, 2019

Elain Harwood, *Space, Hope and Brutalism: English Architecture 1945–75*, London, Yale University Press, 2015

Elain Harwood & James O. Davies, *England's Post-War Listed Buildings*, London, Batsford, 2015

Elain Harwood, *Nottingham Pevsner City Guide*, London, Yale University Press, 2008

Owen Hopkins, *Lost Futures: The Disappearing Architecture of Post-War Britain*, London, Royal Academy of Arts, 2023

Barbara Hulanicki and Martin Pel, *The Biba Years: 1963–1975*, London, V&A Publishing, 2014

James B. Jefferys, *Retail Trading in Britain, 1850–1950: A Study of Trends in Retailing with Special Reference to the Development of Co-operative, Multiple Shop and Department Store Methods of Trading*, Cambridge, Cambridge University Press, 1954

Bill Lancaster, *The Department Store: A Social History*, London, Leicester University Press, 1995

Anca I. Lasc et al. eds. *Architectures of display: department stores and modern retail*, London, Routledge, 2018

Lindsay Lennie, *Scotland's Shops*, Edinburgh, Historic Environment Scotland, 2010

José Manser, *The Joseph Shops, London 1979–88, Eva Jiřičná*, London, Phaidon Press

Kate McIntyre, "The Most 'in' Shops for Gear", *Twentieth Century Architecture* 6, 2002

Kathryn Morrison, *English Shops and Shopping: An Architectural History*, London, Yale University Press, 2003

Kathryn Morrison, *Woolworth's: 100 Years on the High Street*, London, Historic England, 2015

Michael Moss and Alison Turton, *A Legend of Retailing: House of Fraser*. London, Weidenfeld & Nicholson, 1989

Lynn Pearson, *England's Co-operative Movement: An Architectural History*. Liverpool, Liverpool University Press, 2020

Alan Powers, *Modern, The Modern Movement in Britain*. London, Merrell, 2005

Andrew Saint, ed. *Survey of London, volume 53: Oxford Street*, New Haven and London, Yale University Press, 2020

Otto Saumarez Smith, *Boom Cities: Architect Planners and the Politics of Radical Urban Renewal in 1960s Britain*, Oxford, Oxford University Press, 2019

E. Somake and R. Hellberg, *Shops and Stores Today: Their Design Planning and Organisation*, Batsford, 1956

Twentieth Century Society Department Stores campaign: c20society.org.uk/department-stores

David Vernet & Leontine de Wit, *Boutiques and Other Retail Spaces: The Architecture of Seduction*, London, Routledge, 2007

Bryan and Norman Westwood, *Smaller Retail Shops*, London, Architectural Press, 1937

Bryan and Norman Westwood, *The Modern Shop*, London, Architectural Press, 1952

RIGHT Castle House Co-op, Sheffield, George S. Hay, Co-op
Architect's Department, 1959–1964

PICTURE CREDITS

INDEX

The community for modernity.

C20 Society is an independent charity and the guardian of Britain's modern design and architectural heritage.

For over forty years, we've successfully campaigned to save countless landmarks for the nation: from iconic red phone boxes to art deco lidos, brutalist bus stations to pop-art murals, even helping Bankside power station to become the cathedral of art, Tate Modern.

We believe good design enriches lives and contributes towards thriving communities, yet our shared heritage is under threat more than ever before. Each year our casework team tackle thousands of cases and help to secure listed status for remarkable buildings, while our campaigns lead the debate on the built heritage of the future, advancing environmental arguments and championing community solutions.

To find out more and get involved, visit c20society.org.uk

Together, we can protect the best of twentieth and twenty-first century architecture for future generations.